Summer Bridge
Grades 4–5

Editor: Sandra Toland
Layout Design: Tiara Reynolds
Inside Illustrations: Ray Lambert, Wayne Miller
Cover Design: Chasity Rice
Cover Illustration: Wayne Miller

ISBN 978-1-60022-453-9

Table of Contents

How to Use This Book

The *Summer Bridge Math* series is designed to help children improve their mathematical skills during the summer months and between grades. *Summer Bridge Math* includes several extra components to help make your child's study of mathematics easier and more inviting.

For example, an **Assessment** test has been included to help you determine your child's mathematical knowledge and what skills need improvement. Use this test, as well as the **Assessment Analysis**, as a diagnostic tool for those areas in which your child may need extra practice.

Furthermore, the **Incentive Contract** will motivate your child to complete the work in *Summer Bridge Math*. Together, you and your child choose the reward for completing specific sections of the book. Check off the pages that your child has completed, and he or she will have a record of his or her accomplishment.

Examples are included for each new skill that your child will learn. The examples are located in red boxes at the top of the pages. On each page, the directions refer to the example your child needs to complete a specific type of activity.

Assessment

Write the value of each underlined digit.

A. 3,216 _____ 42,506 _____ 823,496 _____

Write the numbers in standard form.

B. five hundred twenty-three _____

C. eighteen thousand four hundred six _____

Find the next number in the pattern below.

D. $3\frac{1}{2}$, 5, $6\frac{1}{2}$, 8, $9\frac{1}{2}$, _____

Solve.

E.
```
    3,412
      826
    1,005
 + 24,117
```
```
   60,000
 - 11,243
```
```
    2,346
 +    239
```

F. $(4 + 9) + (8 + 1) =$ _____ $2 + (4 + 3) =$ _____ $+ 1$

G.
```
    5,875
 x     27
```
```
   42,634
 x     397
```
```
24)3,684
```

H. $8 \times (3 \times 2) =$ _____ $(24 \div 6) + (48 \div 4) =$ _____

Fill in the blank.

I. If the time is now 8:47, what time will it be in 5 hours and 19 minutes? _____

Solve.

J.
```
  $246.04
 +  93.42
```
```
  $874.33
 + 162.04
```
```
   $24.02
 x      6
```
```
3)$93.24
```

© Rainbow Bridge Publishing   Summer Bridge Math RB-904089

Assessment (continued)

Fill in the blanks.

K. 12 inches = _____ feet   1 gallon = _____ quarts

L. 1 hour = _____ minutes   10 decimeters = _____ meter

Solve. Reduce to lowest terms.

M. $\dfrac{2}{3} \times \dfrac{3}{5} =$ _____ $\dfrac{3}{8} \times 2 =$ _____ $\dfrac{2}{12} + \dfrac{4}{12} =$ _____

N. $2\dfrac{3}{8} \times 1\dfrac{2}{7} =$ _____ $2\dfrac{7}{8} \times 1\dfrac{5}{8} =$ _____

O.
$$\begin{array}{r} \dfrac{2}{3} \\ + \\ \dfrac{1}{10} \\ \hline \end{array} \qquad\qquad \begin{array}{r} 8 \\ - \\ \dfrac{5}{6} \\ \hline \end{array}$$

Find the perimeter.

P.

8 m

6 m   7 m

10 m

_____

Find the area.

Q.

4 ft.

3 ft.

_____

Solve.

R. Matt had 84 marbles. If he puts them into groups of 4, how many groups can he make?

_____

4

Assessment Analysis

Assessment Answer Key

A. 3,000; 500; 20,000;
B. 523
C. 18,406
D. 11
E. 29,360; 48,757; 2,585
F. 22, 8
G. 158,625; 16,925,698; 153 r12

H. 48, 16
I. 2:06
J. $339.46; $1,036.37; $144.12; $31.08
K. 1, 4
L. 60, 1
M. $\frac{2}{5}$, $\frac{3}{4}$, $\frac{1}{2}$

N. $3\frac{3}{56}$, $4\frac{43}{56}$
O. $\frac{23}{30}$, $7\frac{1}{6}$
P. 31 m
Q. 12 square feet
R. 21 groups

After reviewing the Assessment test, match the problems answered incorrectly to the corresponding activity pages. Your child should spend extra time on those activities to strengthen his or her math skills.

Diagnostic Problem	Review Section	Review Pages
A., B., C., D.	Numeration	7–9
E., F.	Addition & Subtraction	10–20
G., H.	Multiplication & Division	21–29
I., J.	Time & Money	30–35
K., L.	Measurement	36–42
M., N., O.	Fractions & Decimals	43–64
P., Q.	Geometry	65–74
R.	Problem Solving	83–92

Summer Bridge Math RB-904089

Incentive Contract

	Numeration	√	My Incentive Is:
7	Place Value		
8	Writing Numbers in Standard Form		
9	Whole Number Application		

	Addition and Subtraction	√	My Incentive Is:
10	Addition Strategies		
11	Addition with Regrouping		
12	Column Addition with Regrouping		
13	Adding Larger Numbers		
14	Addition Practice		
15	Rounding and Estimating		
16	Subtraction with Regrouping		
17	Subtracting Larger Numbers		
18	Subtracting Across Zeros		
19	Three- and Four-Digit Mixed Practice		
20	Mixed Practice with Larger Numbers		

	Multiplication and Division	√	My Incentive Is:
21	Multiplying by Two Digits		
22	Multiplying Larger Numbers		
23	Using Grouping Symbols		
24	Basic Division		
25	Dividing with and without Remainders		
26	Dividing by Two Digits		
27	Estimating Quotients		
28	Using Grouping Symbols		
29	Mixed Practice		

	Time and Money	√	My Incentive Is:
30	Telling Time		
31	Elapsed Time		
32	Telling Time Practice		
33	The Value of Money		
34	Adding and Subtracting Money		
35	Estimating Money		

	Measurement	√	My Incentive Is:
36	Length in the Standard System		
37	Length in the Metric System		
38	Capacity in the Standard System		
39	Capacity in the Metric System		
40	Weight in the Standard System		
41	Weight in the Metric System		
42	Time		

	Fractions and Decimals	√	My Incentive Is:
43	Identifying Fractions		
44	Fractions as Words		
45	Simplifying Fractions		
46	Finding Equivalent Fractions		
47	Least Common Denominators		
48	Fractions Equal to and Greater Than One		

49	Improper Fractions		
50	Simplifying Mixed Numbers		
51	Adding Fractions		
52	Subtracting Fractions		
53	Adding Mixed Numbers		
54	Subtracting Mixed Numbers		
55	Multiplying Fractions		
56	Multiplying Fractions by Whole Numbers		
57	Multiplying Mixed Numbers		
58	Visualizing Decimals		
59	Place Value		
60	Tenths and Hundredths		
61	Comparing Decimals		
62	Equivalent Fractions and Decimals		
63	Decimals and Mixed Numbers		
64	Mixed Practice		

	Geometry	√	My Incentive Is:
65	Polygons		
66	Quadrilaterals		
67	Three-Dimensional Objects		
68	Congruent and Similar		
69	Lines of Symmetry		
70	Basic Figures		
71	Angles		
72	Attributes of Shapes		
73	Perimeter		
74	Area		

	Statistics and Graphs	√	My Incentive Is:
75	Tree Diagrams		
76	Graphs		
77	Reading a Schedule		
78	Reading a Thermometer		
79	Finding Probabilities		
80	Finding Probabilities (continued)		
81	Probability Practice		
82	Classifying		

	Problem Solving	√	My Incentive Is:
83	Addition and Subtraction		
84	Multiplication		
85	Division		
86	Money		
87	Measurement		
88	Fractions		
89	Perimeter and Area		
90	Using What We Know		
91	Real-Life Problem Solving		
92	More Real-Life Problem Solving		

Place Value

> In the number below, the underlined digit, 6, is in the hundred thousands place. It has a **place value** of 600,000.

Billions			Millions			Thousands			Ones		
Hundred Billions	Ten Billions	Billions	Hundred Millions	Ten Millions	Millions	Hundred Thousands	Ten Thousands	Thousands	Hundreds	Tens	Ones
5,	5	0	3,	**6**	7	3,	9	8	2		

Study the example and the chart above. Then, write the value of each underlined digit.

A. 3,7<u>4</u>1   4,<u>8</u>25   <u>7</u>5,408

_____   _____   _____

B. 10,<u>8</u>30   <u>1</u>,453,281   <u>2</u>3,486,125

_____   _____   _____

C. 57,20<u>1</u>   7<u>8</u>2,113   1<u>2</u>8,463

_____   _____   _____

D. <u>4</u>47,038,974   3,1<u>7</u>3,414   320,10<u>8</u>,400

_____   _____   _____

E. 725,95<u>3</u>   <u>2</u>64,638,458   6<u>4</u>6,389

_____   _____   _____

F.   Write two 6-digit numbers so that one is exactly one thousand more than the other.

_____

© Rainbow Bridge Publishing   Summer Bridge Math RB-904089

Writing Numbers in Standard Form

> All numbers can be written as either **words** or **numerals**.
> **Example:** seven thousand one hundred twenty-three = **7,123**

Study the example above. Then, write each number in standard form.

A. five thousand six hundred twenty-one _____

B. seven hundred fifty-one thousand nine hundred eight _____

C. thirty-four thousand five hundred two _____

D. eighty-nine thousand six hundred forty-nine _____

E. nine hundred seven thousand one hundred sixty-three _____

F. sixteen thousand five hundred twenty _____

G. ten thousand eighty _____

H. seven hundred four thousand two hundred nine _____

I. one million six thousand five hundred twelve _____

J. seven hundred eighty-one thousand two hundred fifty _____

K. fifty-six thousand nine hundred eight _____

L. twelve million nine hundred seventy-one thousand _____

M. four hundred six million two hundred thirty thousand one _____

N. sixty-four thousand eight hundred three _____

O. ninety-three thousand two _____

Summer Bridge Math RB-904089

Whole Number Application

A small bridge near Melanie's house can hold up to 1,008,500 pounds. Write this number using words.

one million eight thousand five hundred

Study the example above. Then, solve each problem.

A. Write the number that has a 7 in the hundreds place, a 2 in the tens place, and a 3 in the ones place.

_____

B. What 4-digit number has a 7 in the tens place, a 4 in the hundreds place, and a 9 in the thousands place? (The ones place has no value.)

_____

C. The distance from Maggie's house to Jennifer's is one mile, or five thousand two hundred eighty feet. Write the number describing a mile in standard form.

_____

D. In New York Harbor, the Statue of Liberty stands 302 feet high. Write the height in expanded form.

_____

E. In one week, there are six hundred four thousand eight hundred seconds. Write this number in standard form.

_____

F. Leslie's school has eight hundred fifty students, and Mary's school has eight hundred forty-five students. Write the number in standard form that represents the larger student body.

_____

G. Write a 4-digit number greater than 1,562 and less than 1,565.

_____

9

Addition Strategies

To add in **columns**, add the first two numbers. Two plus 7 equals 9. Then, add the last number. Nine plus 4 equals 13.

$$\begin{matrix} \mathbf{2} & \\ \mathbf{7} & \searrow 9 \\ \underline{+\ 4} & \underline{+\ 4} \\ & \mathbf{13} \end{matrix}$$

Study the example above. Then, find each sum.

A.
```
    4          6         11         15         17
    8          5          3         19         14
  + 7        + 2        + 6       + 13       + 12
```

When adding many numbers, follow the **order of operations**. Remember to do the operations in parentheses first.

Example:

$(10 + 8) + 12 = \mathbf{30}$

First find the sum of $10 + 8$.
$10 + 8 = 18$
Then, find the sum of $18 + 12$.
$18 + 12 = 30$

Study the example above. Then, find each sum.

B. $4 + 3 + 8 = $ _____ $(7 + 12) + (16 + 4) = $ _____

C. $(5 + 3) + (9 + 1) = $ _____ $4 + (5 + 18) = $ _____

D. $3 + 2 + 6 = $ _____ $2 + (6 + 13) = $ _____

E. $4 + (3 + 10) = $ _____ $(12 + 14) + (10 + 15) = $ _____

F. $5 + (1 + 6) = $ _____ $(9 + 8) + (16 + 5) = $ _____

G. $3 + 8 + 12 = $ _____ $(10 + 8) + (6 + 1) = $ _____

H. $(4 + 9) + 6 = $ _____ $(9 + 4) + (4 + 8) = $ _____

I. $7 + 3 + 11 = $ _____ $(7 + 0) + (8 + 1) = $ _____

J. $(9 + 2) + (4 + 4) = $ _____ $(4 + 5) + (7 + 6) = $ _____

K. $(7 + 5) + (4 + 3) + 6 = $ _____ $(14 + 2) + (18 + 2) = $ _____

Summer Bridge Math RB-904089

Addition with Regrouping

First, add the ones column. Regroup the tens column.	Then, add the tens column.
$\begin{array}{r} ^1\\ 3\,\mathbf{5}\\ +\,2\,\mathbf{7}\\ \hline \mathbf{2} \end{array}$	$\begin{array}{r} ^1\\ \mathbf{3}\,5\\ +\,\mathbf{2}\,7\\ \hline 6\,2 \end{array}$

Study the example above. Then, find each sum.

A.
$\begin{array}{r} 24\\ +\ 7\\ \hline \end{array}$
$\begin{array}{r} 19\\ +\ 5\\ \hline \end{array}$
$\begin{array}{r} 37\\ +\ 3\\ \hline \end{array}$
$\begin{array}{r} 19\\ +\ 6\\ \hline \end{array}$
$\begin{array}{r} 27\\ +\ 4\\ \hline \end{array}$
$\begin{array}{r} 38\\ +\ 3\\ \hline \end{array}$

B.
$\begin{array}{r} 8\\ +\ 46\\ \hline \end{array}$
$\begin{array}{r} 9\\ +\ 23\\ \hline \end{array}$
$\begin{array}{r} 2\\ +\ 89\\ \hline \end{array}$
$\begin{array}{r} 6\\ +\ 37\\ \hline \end{array}$
$\begin{array}{r} 5\\ +\ 18\\ \hline \end{array}$
$\begin{array}{r} 9\\ +\ 26\\ \hline \end{array}$

C.
$\begin{array}{r} 27\\ +\ 47\\ \hline \end{array}$
$\begin{array}{r} 43\\ +\ 29\\ \hline \end{array}$
$\begin{array}{r} 57\\ +\ 34\\ \hline \end{array}$
$\begin{array}{r} 18\\ +\ 25\\ \hline \end{array}$
$\begin{array}{r} 64\\ +\ 17\\ \hline \end{array}$
$\begin{array}{r} 25\\ +\ 55\\ \hline \end{array}$

D.
$\begin{array}{r} 16\\ +\ 18\\ \hline \end{array}$
$\begin{array}{r} 37\\ +\ 46\\ \hline \end{array}$
$\begin{array}{r} 64\\ +\ 19\\ \hline \end{array}$
$\begin{array}{r} 17\\ +\ 39\\ \hline \end{array}$
$\begin{array}{r} 54\\ +\ 26\\ \hline \end{array}$
$\begin{array}{r} 45\\ +\ 29\\ \hline \end{array}$

E.
$\begin{array}{r} 36\\ +\ 57\\ \hline \end{array}$
$\begin{array}{r} 24\\ +\ 68\\ \hline \end{array}$
$\begin{array}{r} 37\\ +\ 43\\ \hline \end{array}$
$\begin{array}{r} 66\\ +\ 29\\ \hline \end{array}$
$\begin{array}{r} 53\\ +\ 39\\ \hline \end{array}$
$\begin{array}{r} 74\\ +\ 19\\ \hline \end{array}$

F.
$\begin{array}{r} 19\\ +\ 35\\ \hline \end{array}$
$\begin{array}{r} 26\\ +\ 47\\ \hline \end{array}$
$\begin{array}{r} 18\\ +\ 77\\ \hline \end{array}$
$\begin{array}{r} 36\\ +\ 19\\ \hline \end{array}$
$\begin{array}{r} 28\\ +\ 16\\ \hline \end{array}$
$\begin{array}{r} 46\\ +\ 39\\ \hline \end{array}$

G.
$\begin{array}{r} 58\\ +\ 26\\ \hline \end{array}$
$\begin{array}{r} 29\\ +\ 45\\ \hline \end{array}$
$\begin{array}{r} 46\\ +\ 39\\ \hline \end{array}$
$\begin{array}{r} 55\\ +\ 29\\ \hline \end{array}$
$\begin{array}{r} 86\\ +\ 16\\ \hline \end{array}$
$\begin{array}{r} 79\\ +\ 19\\ \hline \end{array}$

Column Addition with Regrouping

Study the examples on pages 10 and 11. Then, find each sum.

A.
```
   12        35        34        50        13
   14        30        22        42        62
 + 34       + 6      + 60      + 56      + 47
```

B.
```
  354       132       253       624       450
   41        30        34        13        26
 + 24      + 77      + 61      + 38      + 61
```

C.
```
  214       324       624       734       344
  136       241       131       230       103
 + 324     + 345     + 410     + 373     + 624
```

D.
```
 3,246     6,324     2,354     3,413     2,436
 4,131     1,347     1,034     6,341     4,064
+ 2,134   + 2,341   + 4,316   + 7,642   + 1,483
```

E.
```
 2,341     7,341     1,209     5,442     1,023
 3,456     2,683     3,416     1,330     3,542
 1,348     2,134     1,221     1,342     2,134
+ 2,367   + 2,011   + 1,354   + 6,341   + 7,241
```

F.
```
 3,541     1,302     1,463     3,621     4,621
 1,204     4,211     4,231     1,241     3,024
 2,301     5,140     3,141     2,314     3,647
+ 20,143  + 35,333  + 53,410  + 44,213  + 61,213
```

Summer Bridge Math RB-904089

Adding Larger Numbers

rightaddition and subtraction

First, add the ones column.	Next, add the tens column.	Then, add the hundreds column.	Last, add the thousands column.
1	1	1 1	1 1
2,5**37**	2,5**3**7	**2,5**37	**2,5**37
+ 4,7**24**	+ 4,7**2**4	+4,**7**24	+**4,7**24
1	**61**	**261**	**7,261**

Study the example above. Then, find each sum.

A. 4,510 + 4,689	7,166 + 5,622	2,198 + 2,516	6,043 + 6,428	4,025 + 1,298
B. 1,889 + 8,458	7,168 + 2,362	5,530 + 9,022	6,046 + 5,539	2,270 + 8,696
C. 8,979 + 3,285	5,328 + 5,991	6,135 + 1,170	2,030 + 6,537	1,947 + 1,835
D. 7,564 + 5,167	3,504 + 1,606	3,044 + 4,492	5,013 + 8,362	3,501 + 4,530
E. 2,044 + 5,367	9,600 + 8,664	7,187 + 3,436	2,385 + 5,652	3,643 + 7,244
F. 28,734 + 60,828	55,877 + 66,244	46,780 + 46,687	65,464 + 98,795	24,336 + 55,051
G. 26,634 + 24,997	75,019 + 82,226	66,777 + 19,607	44,041 + 17,092	70,292 + 40,323

Summer Bridge Math RB-904089

Addition Practice

Study the examples on pages 10, 11, and 13. Then, find each sum.

A.

430	754	174	427	786
978	904	370	140	442
+ 557	+ 723	+ 254	+ 222	+ 209

B.

4,210	9,012	5,816	6,318	2,477
9,733	3,923	1,116	8,833	4,841
+ 1,358	+ 7,725	+ 6,676	+ 7,381	+ 5,713

C.

136	7,164	419	2,342	54,331
435	2,300	6,304	49,534	23,097
257	4,671	2,783	14,735	24,781
+ 375	+ 9,610	+ 8,901	+ 58,651	+ 25,672

D.

253	475	2,742	4,432	4,825
430	234	7,463	9,857	43,029
249	987	4,687	1,248	12,064
475	178	2,115	7,824	16,753
+ 958	+ 572	+ 2,950	+ 5,432	+ 58,439

E.

476	546	1,564	15,761	4,567
578	4,789	12,457	27,892	18,796
483	4,871	55,793	489,741	124
473	1,753	6,782	156,474	34,897
571	154	34,584	152,767	123
+ 128	+ 1,674	+ 3,487	+ 8,243	+ 4,576

Summer Bridge Math RB-904089

Rounding and Estimating

342 rounds to 300	Look to the right of the first number. If that number is 5 or greater, round up. If that number is 4 or less, round down.

Round each number to the greatest place value position.

A. 35   78   21   62

_____   _____   _____   _____

B. 175   380   218   3,462

_____   _____   _____   _____

C. 5,807   9,462   23,940   51,998

_____   _____   _____   _____

Round each number to the greatest place value position. Then, add for the estimated sum. The first one has been done for you.

D.
$$38 \approx 40$$
$$+ 24 \approx + 20$$
$$60$$

$$78$$
$$+ 24$$

$$64$$
$$+ 39$$

$$28$$
$$+ 14$$

E.
$$179$$
$$+ 34$$

$$782$$
$$+ 136$$

$$149$$
$$+ 29$$

$$1,364$$
$$+ 288$$

F.
$$4,624$$
$$+ 136$$

$$298$$
$$+ 642$$

$$7,540$$
$$+ 8,429$$

$$17,486$$
$$+ 13,244$$

Summer Bridge Math RB-904089

Subtraction with Regrouping

Regroup the tens column. Four tens and 6 ones equals 3 tens and 16 ones. Subtract the ones column.	Regroup the hundreds column. Four hundreds and 3 tens equals 3 hundreds and 13 tens. Subtract the tens column.	Subtract the hundreds column.
$$\begin{array}{r} \overset{3}{4}\overset{1}{\cancel{4}}6 \\ -\ \ 57 \\ \hline 9 \end{array}$$	$$\begin{array}{r} \overset{3}{\cancel{4}}\overset{13}{\cancel{4}}\overset{1}{6} \\ -\ \ 57 \\ \hline 89 \end{array}$$	$$\begin{array}{r} \overset{3}{\cancel{4}}\overset{13}{\cancel{4}}\overset{1}{6} \\ -\ \ 57 \\ \hline 389 \end{array}$$

Study the example above. Then, find each difference.

A.

$$\begin{array}{r} 129 \\ -\ 62 \\ \hline \end{array} \qquad \begin{array}{r} 204 \\ -\ 43 \\ \hline \end{array} \qquad \begin{array}{r} 215 \\ -\ 91 \\ \hline \end{array} \qquad \begin{array}{r} 146 \\ -\ 77 \\ \hline \end{array} \qquad \begin{array}{r} 318 \\ -\ 36 \\ \hline \end{array} \qquad \begin{array}{r} 618 \\ -\ 51 \\ \hline \end{array}$$

B.

$$\begin{array}{r} 507 \\ -\ 82 \\ \hline \end{array} \qquad \begin{array}{r} 238 \\ -\ 43 \\ \hline \end{array} \qquad \begin{array}{r} 357 \\ -\ 69 \\ \hline \end{array} \qquad \begin{array}{r} 466 \\ -\ 82 \\ \hline \end{array} \qquad \begin{array}{r} 683 \\ -\ 92 \\ \hline \end{array} \qquad \begin{array}{r} 908 \\ -\ 17 \\ \hline \end{array}$$

C.

$$\begin{array}{r} 229 \\ -\ 46 \\ \hline \end{array} \qquad \begin{array}{r} 837 \\ -\ 45 \\ \hline \end{array} \qquad \begin{array}{r} 687 \\ -\ 94 \\ \hline \end{array} \qquad \begin{array}{r} 548 \\ -\ 93 \\ \hline \end{array} \qquad \begin{array}{r} 936 \\ -\ 64 \\ \hline \end{array} \qquad \begin{array}{r} 434 \\ -\ 92 \\ \hline \end{array}$$

D.

$$\begin{array}{r} 378 \\ -\ 99 \\ \hline \end{array} \qquad \begin{array}{r} 604 \\ -\ 17 \\ \hline \end{array} \qquad \begin{array}{r} 476 \\ -\ 77 \\ \hline \end{array} \qquad \begin{array}{r} 611 \\ -\ 42 \\ \hline \end{array} \qquad \begin{array}{r} 964 \\ -\ 37 \\ \hline \end{array} \qquad \begin{array}{r} 137 \\ -\ 79 \\ \hline \end{array}$$

E.

$$\begin{array}{r} 100 \\ -\ 48 \\ \hline \end{array} \qquad \begin{array}{r} 423 \\ -\ 78 \\ \hline \end{array} \qquad \begin{array}{r} 630 \\ -\ 15 \\ \hline \end{array} \qquad \begin{array}{r} 224 \\ -\ 92 \\ \hline \end{array} \qquad \begin{array}{r} 576 \\ -\ 89 \\ \hline \end{array} \qquad \begin{array}{r} 731 \\ -\ 20 \\ \hline \end{array}$$

F.

$$\begin{array}{r} 647 \\ -\ 87 \\ \hline \end{array} \qquad \begin{array}{r} 502 \\ -\ 35 \\ \hline \end{array} \qquad \begin{array}{r} 157 \\ -\ 92 \\ \hline \end{array} \qquad \begin{array}{r} 367 \\ -\ 48 \\ \hline \end{array} \qquad \begin{array}{r} 960 \\ -\ 56 \\ \hline \end{array} \qquad \begin{array}{r} 729 \\ -\ 56 \\ \hline \end{array}$$

Summer Bridge Math RB-904089

Subtracting Larger Numbers

addition and subtraction

Study the example on page 16. Then, find each difference.

A.	3,186 − 2,123	7,964 − 1,280	6,522 − 4,910	5,885 − 5,347	6,733 − 5,942
B.	9,901 − 4,576	9,483 − 7,376	8,436 − 4,987	6,625 − 1,784	5,167 − 1,170
C.	85,350 − 4,383	87,401 − 9,289	81,761 − 815	97,342 − 5,052	68,797 − 8,749
D.	60,721 − 9,485	66,595 − 4,684	74,118 − 3,982	33,688 − 1,962	97,810 − 5,219
E.	90,646 − 86,247	75,460 − 16,933	46,054 − 13,241	16,470 − 14,549	84,192 − 39,559
F.	99,543 − 54,109	79,583 − 58,149	25,911 − 20,300	51,313 − 46,851	99,564 − 98,300

Summer Bridge Math RB-904089

Subtracting Across Zeros

Regrouping with zeros is the same as regrouping with any number. Just keep regrouping from right to left until you reach a whole number.

Study the example on page 16. Then, find each difference.

A.	20 − 9	70 − 18	150 − 28	100 − 37
B.	200 − 45	3,000 − 298	700 − 241	900 − 352
C.	5,000 − 747	600 − 189	1,000 − 256	2,000 − 468
D.	800 − 641	400 − 133	3,000 − 724	1,800 − 532
E.	2,700 − 908	1,900 − 630	75,000 − 299	70,000 − 12,342
F.	68,000 − 2,498	30,000 − 18,437	60,000 − 9,427	5,000 − 1,289
G.	6,000 − 1,597	84,000 − 2,698	13,000 − 6,871	10,000 − 5,982

Summer Bridge Math RB-904089

Three- and Four-Digit Mixed Practice

Study the examples on pages 11–18. Then, solve each problem.

A.
231	461	647	513	767	354
+ 762	+ 329	+ 282	+ 864	+ 350	+ 937

B.
598	318	667	467	873	248
+ 324	+ 487	+ 571	+ 664	+168	+ 367

C.
317	466	504	846	496	651
+ 218	+ 871	+ 947	+ 516	+ 570	+ 947

D.
597	618	381	947	265	3,410
− 162	− 209	− 159	− 763	− 177	− 348

E.
1,471	2,284	1,248	1,420	2,019	1,400
− 254	− 743	− 726	− 803	− 249	− 621

F.
2,000	3,164	1,907	2,546	1,644	1,762
− 637	− 726	− 267	− 467	− 795	− 781

19

Mixed Practice with Larger Numbers

Study the examples on pages 11–18. Then, solve each problem.

A.

1,676	3,873	6,824	4,357	2,164	5,324
+ 243	+ 129	+ 359	+ 937	+ 396	+ 907

B.

3,674	1,786	4,364	7,354	6,537	2,561
+ 1,218	+ 316	+ 7,129	+ 4,166	+ 2,845	+ 3,674

C.

5,637	8,371	2,687	4,698	5,307	7,543
+ 6,631	+ 4,929	+ 4,982	+ 1,279	+ 6,379	+ 3,178

D.

3,217	2,346	7,652	6,718	2,736	9,861
− 304	− 273	− 419	− 509	− 918	− 7,539

E.

2,647	1,966	4,645	7,668	3,744	8,482
− 1,328	− 1,248	− 3,927	− 2,880	− 1,656	− 4,027

F.

27,437	63,476	56,073	36,427	42,578	79,483
− 3,129	− 4,147	− 3,747	− 4,686	− 8,724	− 5,446

Multiplying by Two Digits

multiplication and division

Multiply the ones. Regroup as you multiply across.	Multiply the tens. Regroup as you multiply across.	Add.
⁴ ²¹ **8,743** x 4**6** **52,458**	² ¹¹ **8,743** x 4 6 5 2 , 4 5 8 **349,720**	8,743 x 46 ¹¹ ₁**52,458** +**349,720** **402,178**

Study the example above. Then, multiply.

A.
3,601	5,015	1,264	2,641
x 15	x 21	x 25	x 41

B.
3,216	2,643	3,180	8,436
x 47	x 39	x 13	x 42

C.
1,345	3,406	5,348	2,648
x 62	x 21	x 51	x 18

D.
9,018	2,667	1,064	6,912
x 54	x 36	x 28	x 46

© Rainbow Bridge Publishing Summer Bridge Math RB-904089

Multiplying Larger Numbers

multiplication and division

Study the example on page 21. Then, multiply.

A.
$$
\begin{array}{r} 925 \\ \times\,883 \\ \hline \end{array}
\qquad
\begin{array}{r} 963 \\ \times\,500 \\ \hline \end{array}
\qquad
\begin{array}{r} 916 \\ \times\,648 \\ \hline \end{array}
\qquad
\begin{array}{r} 157 \\ \times\,616 \\ \hline \end{array}
$$

B.
$$
\begin{array}{r} 884 \\ \times\,971 \\ \hline \end{array}
\qquad
\begin{array}{r} 434 \\ \times\,251 \\ \hline \end{array}
\qquad
\begin{array}{r} 754 \\ \times\,173 \\ \hline \end{array}
\qquad
\begin{array}{r} 516 \\ \times\,688 \\ \hline \end{array}
$$

C.
$$
\begin{array}{r} 9{,}183 \\ \times\,\;\;217 \\ \hline \end{array}
\qquad
\begin{array}{r} 7{,}736 \\ \times\,\;\;360 \\ \hline \end{array}
\qquad
\begin{array}{r} 6{,}949 \\ \times\,\;\;239 \\ \hline \end{array}
\qquad
\begin{array}{r} 1{,}162 \\ \times\,\;\;495 \\ \hline \end{array}
$$

D.
$$
\begin{array}{r} 1{,}175 \\ \times\,\;\;404 \\ \hline \end{array}
\qquad
\begin{array}{r} 2{,}748 \\ \times\,\;\;462 \\ \hline \end{array}
\qquad
\begin{array}{r} 5{,}471 \\ \times\,\;\;376 \\ \hline \end{array}
\qquad
\begin{array}{r} 8{,}314 \\ \times\,\;\;574 \\ \hline \end{array}
$$

Summer Bridge Math RB-904089

© Rainbow Bridge Publishing

$(2 \times 5) \times 3 =$ _____

$(3 \times 1) + 6 =$ _____

Think: $2 \times 5 = 10$ and $10 \times 3 = 30$. Therefore, 30 is the final **product**. Think: $3 \times 1 = 3$ and $3 + 6 = 9$. Therefore, 9 is the final **solution**.

Study the examples above. Then, solve each problem.

A. $(5 \times 4) \times 2 =$ _____

B. $(7 \times 4) \times 5 =$ _____

C. $1 \times (8 \times 3) =$ _____

D. $(3 \times 3) \times (1 \times 4) =$ _____

E. $(7 \times 3) \times (1 \times 2) =$ _____

F. $(3 \times 7) + 9 =$ _____

G. $(7 \times 3) + 5 =$ _____

H. $9 - (6 \times 1) =$ _____

I. $(5 \times 7) - 10 =$ _____

J. $(6 \times 10) - 5 =$ _____

$(3 \times 1) \times 5 =$ _____

$2 \times (5 \times 3) =$ _____

$3 \times (6 \times 8) =$ _____

$(2 \times 4) \times (1 \times 5) =$ _____

$(9 \times 2) \times (1 \times 6) =$ _____

$(4 \times 5) + (6 \times 2) =$ _____

$8 + (2 \times 4) =$ _____

$(8 \times 3) - 12 =$ _____

$(3 \times 3) + 8 =$ _____

$(3 \times 6) + (5 \times 3) =$ _____

Basic Division

$$
\begin{array}{r}
61 \\
6\overline{)366} \\
-36 \quad\longleftarrow \quad 6 \times 6 = 36 \text{ Subtract 36 from 36. Bring down the 6.} \\
06 \\
-6 \quad\longleftarrow \quad 6 \times 1 = 6 \text{ Subtract 6 from 6.} \\
0
\end{array}
$$

Study the example above. Then, divide.

A. $6\overline{)336}$ $\quad$ $4\overline{)108}$ $\quad$ $9\overline{)585}$ $\quad$ $6\overline{)522}$ $\quad$ $9\overline{)738}$

B. $8\overline{)216}$ $\quad$ $7\overline{)483}$ $\quad$ $8\overline{)728}$ $\quad$ $5\overline{)235}$ $\quad$ $4\overline{)312}$

C. $3\overline{)276}$ $\quad$ $2\overline{)284}$ $\quad$ $4\overline{)764}$ $\quad$ $7\overline{)441}$ $\quad$ $8\overline{)656}$

D. $9\overline{)252}$ $\quad$ $7\overline{)301}$ $\quad$ $3\overline{)288}$ $\quad$ $2\overline{)194}$ $\quad$ $6\overline{)144}$

E. $5\overline{)115}$ $\quad$ $4\overline{)348}$ $\quad$ $9\overline{)756}$ $\quad$ $7\overline{)476}$ $\quad$ $2\overline{)116}$

Summer Bridge Math RB-904089

Dividing with and without Remainders

$$
\begin{array}{r}
622\ \text{r5} \\
7\ )\overline{4,359} \\
\end{array}
$$

7)4,359

  - 42 ← 7 x 6 = 42 Subtract 42 from 43. Bring down the 5.

    15

  - 14 ← 7 x 2 = 14 Subtract 14 from 15. Bring down the 9.

    19

  - 14 ← 7 x 2 = 14 Subtract 14 from 19.

    5   Because 5 is less than 7, the **remainder** is 5.

Study the example above. Then, divide.

A.   2)2,482   6)2,412   3)1,797   4)2,616   8)1,632

B.   5)3,571   4)3,691   7)7,198   2)8,617   3)2,794

    Summer Bridge Math RB-904089

Dividing by Two Digits

```
        136 r4
18) 2,452        ←——  18 x 1 = 18  Subtract 18 from 24. Bring down the 5.
   - 18
     65          ←——  18 x 3 = 54  Subtract 54 from 65. Bring down the 2.
   - 54
    112          ←——  18 x 6 = 108  Subtract 108 from 112.
   - 108
      4                Because 4 is less than 18, the remainder is 4.
```

Study the example above. Then, divide.

A.   37) 4,072   81) 4,455   69) 4,740   52) 3,486

B.   46) 2,408   21) 1,240   56) 6,721

C.   24) 1,200   82) 5,832   14) 5,604   35) 1,610

D.   90) 1,445   67) 5,655   25) 1,275

Summer Bridge Math RB-904089

Estimating Quotients

multiplication and division

$$4\overline{)62} \qquad \text{Think:} \quad 4\overline{)60} \qquad \text{then,} \quad \begin{array}{r} 15 \\ 4\overline{)60} \\ -4 \\ \hline 20 \\ -20 \\ \hline 0 \end{array}$$

The **estimated quotient** is 15.

Study the example above. Then, find the estimate of each quotient.

A. $9\overline{)47}$ $3\overline{)87}$ $4\overline{)79}$

B. $2\overline{)61}$ $4\overline{)43}$ $5\overline{)62}$

C. $2\overline{)99}$ $8\overline{)75}$ $5\overline{)13}$

D. $6\overline{)58}$ $9\overline{)94}$ $5\overline{)88}$

E. $4\overline{)122}$ $4\overline{)149}$ $6\overline{)269}$

F. $2\overline{)552}$ $8\overline{)813}$ $3\overline{)880}$

       Summer Bridge Math RB-904089

Using Grouping Symbols

multiplication and division

$(16 \div 2) \div 2 =$ _____

$(9 \div 3) + 8 =$ _____

Think: $16 \div 2 = 8$, and $8 \div 2 = 4$. Therefore, 4 is the final solution. Think: $9 \div 3 = 3$, and $3 + 8 = 11$. Therefore, 11 is the final solution.

TIP: Pay special attention to the signs (+, −, or ÷).

Study the examples above. Then, solve each problem.

A. $(9 \div 3) \div 1 =$ _____ $(18 \div 6) \div 3 =$ _____

B. $(48 \div 12) \div 2 =$ _____ $3 \div (27 \div 9) =$ _____

C. $(24 \div 4) \div 3 =$ _____ $(60 \div 10) \div 3 =$ _____

D. $(32 \div 4) \div 8 =$ _____ $(45 \div 3) \div 3 =$ _____

E. $(28 \div 7) \div 2 =$ _____ $(36 \div 4) \div 3 =$ _____

F. $(2 \div 1) + (8 \div 4) =$ _____ $(32 \div 4) + 3 =$ _____

G. $(49 \div 7) - 5 =$ _____ $(42 \div 6) + (30 \div 5) =$ _____

H. $(72 \div 9) + 8 =$ _____ $(96 \div 12) + 9 =$ _____

I. $(20 \div 5) + (16 \div 4) =$ _____ $(56 \div 7) \div (20 \div 10) =$ _____

J. $(63 \div 9) \div (21 \div 3) =$ _____ $(40 \div 8) + 5 =$ _____

28

Summer Bridge Math RB-904089   © Rainbow Bridge Publishing

Mixed Practice

```
       47 r1
   4 )189  ←——  These numbers
    -16           are the same.
     29
    -28
      1
```

To check your answer:
```
         47
        x 4
        188
       + 1   ←—— Add the remainder here.
        189
```

Study the example above. Then, divide. Multiply to check your answer.

A.   4)419   3)956   2)167

B.   5)6,487   9)5,075   7)5,521

C.   8)7,911   4)1,675   3)5,539

© Rainbow Bridge Publishing

Summer Bridge Math RB-904089

Telling Time

Minutes after the hour—Start at the 12 and count the minutes after the hour.

20 minutes past 10:00 or 10:20

42 minutes after 10:00 or 10:42

Minutes before the hour—Start at the 12 and count the minutes before the hour. Tell time this way when it is more than 30 minutes past the hour.

50 minutes after 4:00 or 10 minutes before 5:00 or 4:50

40 minutes after 2:00 or 20 minutes before 3:00 or 2:40

Study the examples above. Then, write each time.

A.

_____ minutes

after _____

B.

_____ minutes

after _____

C.

_____ minutes

after _____

D.

_____ minutes

after _____

E.

_____ minutes

after _____

F.

_____ minutes

after _____

G.

_____ minutes

after _____

Summer Bridge Math RB-904089

Elapsed Time

10:42

To find out what time it will be later, add the **elapsed** time to the current time. **Example:** It is 10:42. What time will it be in 1 hour and 28 minutes? One hour later than 10:42 is 11:42. Twenty-eight minutes later than 11:42 is 12:10.

12:10

Study the example above. Then, find each time.

A. 20 minutes later

_____

45 minutes later

_____

25 minutes later

_____

B. 30 minutes later

_____

15 minutes before

_____

40 minutes before

_____

C. 20 minutes after 6:35 _____   15 minutes after 7:50 _____

D. 1 hour and 5 minutes before 3:00   1 hour and 35 minutes after 11:15

_____   _____

E. 40 minutes after 2:15 _____   35 minutes before 4:20 _____

F. 50 minutes after 1:55 _____   30 minutes after 3:20 _____

G. How many hours are left in the morning if it is 10:00 A.M.? _____

31

Telling Time Practice

Study the examples on pages 30 and 31. Then, find each time.

A. What time will it be in 2 hours and 15 minutes?

_____

B. What time was it 5 hours and 30 minutes earlier?

_____

C. What time was it 3 hours earlier?

_____

D. What time will it be in 3 hours and 45 minutes?

_____

E. What time was it 4 hours and 15 minutes earlier?

_____

F. What time will it be in 1 hour and 30 minutes?

_____

G. What time was it 2 hours and 30 minutes earlier?

_____

H. What time will it be in 6 hours and 15 minutes?

_____

I. Ryan left 25 minutes before his soccer lesson. If his soccer lesson was at 2:45 P.M., what time did Ryan leave?

_____

J. Terry has 50 minutes left to shop before the mall closes. It is 9:05 P.M. What time does the mall close?

_____

K. Amber arrived 25 minutes early for her dentist appointment. If her appointment was scheduled for 7:45 A.M., what time did Amber arrive at the dentist's office?

_____

L. Cassie left the movie at 9:15 P.M. She stopped for 30 minutes to eat dinner. Then, she drove home in 15 minutes. What time did Cassie get home?

_____

Summer Bridge Math RB-904089

The Value of Money

| 50¢ or $0.50 | 25¢ or $0.25 | 10¢ or $0.10 | 5¢ or $0.05 | 1¢ or $0.01 |

2 dollars and 21 cents = $2.21

forty-four dollars and seventy-two cents = $44.72

Study the coin values and the examples above. Then, write the decimal numbers for each amount.

A. 6 dollars and 35 cents = $ _____   9 dollars and 27 cents = $ _____

B. 4 dollars and 42 cents = $ _____   5 dollars and 75 cents = $ _____

C. 7 dollars and 61 cents = $ _____   3 dollars and 84 cents = $ _____

D. Fifteen dollars and twenty-two cents   = $ _____

E. Twenty-four dollars and thirty-four cents = $ _____

F. Fifty-seven dollars and nineteen cents   = $ _____

G. Seventy dollars and ninety-nine cents   = $ _____

H. Thirty-five dollars and twenty-nine cents = $ _____

I. Eighty-five dollars and fifteen cents   = $ _____

J. What is the total value of 3 quarters and 5 nickels?

_____

K. What is the total value of 9 dimes, 2 nickels, and 7 pennies?

_____

L. What is the total value of 4 one-dollar bills, 3 quarters, 4 dimes, and 2 pennies?

_____

M. What is the total value of 3 five-dollar bills, 4 dimes, 1 nickel, and 8 pennies?

_____

N. What is the total value of 6 ten-dollar bills, 5 dimes, 1 nickel, and 7 pennies?

_____

O. What is the total value of 5 quarters, 2 dimes, and 1 nickel?

_____

Summer Bridge Math RB-904089

Adding and Subtracting Money

Adding and subtracting money is like adding and subtracting any other numbers. You must pay close attention to the decimal. Keep the decimal two places from the right. Regroup as needed.

```
  $7.75
+  6.22
 $13.97
```

Study the example above. Then, solve each problem.

A.
```
  $3.42        $9.71        $13.42        $18.25
+  5.84      +  6.22      +  15.91      +  18.74
```

B.
```
 $25.93       $57.31       $63.31       $148.22
+ 17.86      + 32.85      + 49.56      + 131.98
```

C.
```
$356.82      $624.12      $764.02      $495.30
+ 281.90     + 534.18     + 639.14     + 308.21
```

D.
```
 $45.31       $64.21       $38.26       $138.64
- 24.85      - 46.94      - 29.14      -  97.89
```

E.
```
$328.06      $421.49      $792.08      $974.33
- 217.94     - 168.50     - 488.00     - 498.17
```

F.
```
$807.00      $604.31      $336.34      $575.00
- 566.59     - 328.98     - 207.81     - 284.99
```

G.
```
$942.00      $817.40      $699.50      $730.02
- 686.41     + 163.28     - 259.99     + 264.19
```

H. John's shirt cost $17.85. He paid with a $20.00 bill. How much change did he receive? _____

Estimating Money

Round each dollar amount to the closest whole dollar. Then, solve.

$9.84   Think: $9.84 is closest to $10.00, and $3.31 is
+ 3.31   closest to $3.00; therefore, $10.00 + $3.00 = $13.00.

Examples:

$$\begin{array}{r} \$12.75 \\ -\ \ 9.08 \end{array} \longrightarrow \begin{array}{r} \$13.00 \\ -\ \ 9.00 \\ \hline \$\ \ 4.00 \end{array} \qquad \begin{array}{r} \$6.52 \\ \times\ \ \ 5 \end{array} \longrightarrow \begin{array}{r} \$7.00 \\ \times\ \ \ 5 \\ \hline \$35.00 \end{array} \qquad 4)\overline{\$7.95} \longrightarrow \begin{array}{r} \$2.00 \\ 4)\overline{\$8.00} \\ -8\ \downarrow \\ \hline 0.00 \end{array}$$

Study the examples above. Then, solve each problem.

A
$$\begin{array}{r} \$5.21 \\ +\ 3.84 \end{array} \qquad \begin{array}{r} \$9.43 \\ +\ 6.09 \end{array} \qquad \begin{array}{r} \$7.92 \\ +\ 5.14 \end{array} \qquad \begin{array}{r} \$15.29 \\ +\ 12.85 \end{array}$$

B.
$$\begin{array}{r} \$27.81 \\ +\ 16.52 \end{array} \qquad \begin{array}{r} \$57.03 \\ +\ 38.94 \end{array} \qquad \begin{array}{r} \$9.78 \\ -\ 5.22 \end{array} \qquad \begin{array}{r} \$11.37 \\ -\ 5.22 \end{array}$$

C.
$$\begin{array}{r} \$19.40 \\ -\ 12.06 \end{array} \qquad \begin{array}{r} \$23.45 \\ -\ 19.00 \end{array} \qquad \begin{array}{r} \$49.68 \\ -\ 30.88 \end{array} \qquad \begin{array}{r} \$78.49 \\ -\ 56.81 \end{array}$$

D.
$$\begin{array}{r} \$7.96 \\ \times\ \ \ \ 4 \end{array} \qquad \begin{array}{r} \$16.47 \\ \times\ \ \ \ 3 \end{array} \qquad \begin{array}{r} \$26.41 \\ \times\ \ \ \ 5 \end{array} \qquad \begin{array}{r} \$42.68 \\ \times\ \ \ \ 9 \end{array}$$

E.
$$6)\overline{\$24.32} \qquad 8)\overline{\$39.95} \qquad 3)\overline{\$9.08} \qquad 5)\overline{\$10.45}$$

35

© Rainbow Bridge Publishing   Summer Bridge Math RB-904089

Length in the Standard System

These are equivalent units of **length** in the standard system:

Since 12 inches = 1 foot,
24 inches = 2 feet.

12 inches (in.) = 1 foot (ft.)
3 feet (ft.) = 1 yard (yd.)
1,760 yards (yd.) = 1 mile (mi.)

Study the equivalents above. Then, find each missing number.

A. 24 in. = _____ ft. 6 ft. = _____ in. 8 yd. = _____ ft.

B. 2 yd. = _____ ft. 3 mi. = _____ yd. 45 ft. = _____ yd.

C. 4 ft. = _____ in. 27 ft. = _____ yd. 60 in. = _____ ft.

D. 3,520 yd. = _____ mi. 6 yd. = _____ ft. 5 ft. = _____ in.

E. 7 ft. = _____ in. 30 ft. = _____ yd. 4 mi. = _____ yd.

Answer each question.

F. Peter needs 42 feet of string for his project. How many yards should he buy?

G. Ruby needs 144 inches of ribbon. How many yards does she need to buy?

H. Jamie buys 6 yards of fabric. How many feet of fabric does she have?

I. Juan is 5 feet and 6 inches tall. How many inches tall is Juan?

Length in the Metric System

> These are equivalent units of **length** in the metric system:
>
> Since 1 m = 100 cm,
> 3 m = 300 cm.
>
> 1 centimeter (cm) = 10 millimeters (mm)
> 1 decimeter (dm) = 10 centimeters (cm)
> 1 meter (m) = 100 centimeters (cm)
> 1 kilometer (km) = 1,000 meters
> 10 decimeters = 1 meter

Measure each line segment to the nearest centimeter.

A. _____ _____   _____ _____

B. _____ _____   _____ _____

C. ____ _____   _____ _____

Study the equivalents above. Then, find each missing number.

D. 3 km = _____ m	5 cm = _____ mm	2 m = _____ cm
E. 3 m = _____ dm	2,000 m = _____ km	500 cm = _____ m
F. 30 mm = _____ cm	5 km = _____ m	_____ m = 400 cm
G. _____ cm = 7 dm	2.5 m = _____ cm	_____ m = 3.5 km

Circle the most sensible measurement.

H.   height of a front door: length of a thumb:

            2 cm, 2 m, 2 km   3 cm, 3 dm, 3 m

© Rainbow Bridge Publishing

Summer Bridge Math RB-904089

Capacity in the Standard System

These are equivalent units of **capacity** in the standard system:

Since 1 quart = 2 pints,
2 quarts = 4 pints

1 tablespoon (tbs.) = 3 teaspoons (tsp.)
1 pint (pt.) = 2 cups (c.)
1 quart (qt.) = 2 pints (pt.)
1 gallon (gal.) = 4 quarts (qt.)

Study the equivalents above. Then, find each missing number.

A. 32 qt. = _____ gal.   5 pt. = _____ c.   16 gal. = _____ qt.

B. 7 gal. = _____ qt.   4 tbs. = _____ tsp.   34 c. = _____ pt.

C. 32 pt. = _____ c.   16 c. = _____ pt.   12 tbs. = _____ tsp.

D. 10 tbs. = _____ tsp.   15 pt. = _____ c.   11 gal. = _____ qt.

E. 4 c. = _____ pt.   36 tsp. = _____ tbs.   28 qt. = _____ gal.

Answer each question.

F. Jordan is making lemonade for his party. He uses 7 quarts of water in his recipe. How many pints of water does he need?

G. Josie's pie recipe calls for 6 pints of chopped fruit. How many cups of chopped fruit does she need if she doubles her recipe?

H. Sam needs 28 quarts of hot chocolate for the party. How many gallons should he buy?

I. Marcy bottles 17 gallons of root beer and 12 gallons of punch. She sells her drinks in quart bottles. How many bottles does she need?

Summer Bridge Math RB-904089

Capacity in the Metric System

A **milliliter** (mL) is used to measure the capacity of very small amounts. A **liter** (L) is used to measure the capacity of large amounts.	1 L = 1,000 mL To change liters to milliliters, multiply by 1,000. To change milliliters to liters, divide by 1,000. Since 1 L = 1,000 mL, 7 L = 7,000 mL

Would you choose milliliters or liters to measure the following?

A. tea in a teapot _____   water in a bathtub _____   paint in a can _____

B. juice in a glass_____   water in a lake _____   oil in a teaspoon _____

C. gasoline in a tank _____   soup in a bowl _____   juice from a lemon _____

Study the example above. Then, find each missing number.

D. 2 L = _____ mL   3,000 mL = _____ L   9,000 mL = _____ L

E. 2.5 L = _____ mL   6.7 L = _____ L   3,500 mL = _____ L

F. 7,000 mL = _____ L   5 L = _____ mL   4.5 L = _____ mL

Choose milliliters or liters to complete each sentence.

G. The dog drank about 600 _____ of water.

H. A swimming pool holds about 80,000 _____ of water.

I. The jar holds about 750 _____ of oil.

Summer Bridge Math RB-904089

Weight in the Standard System

> These are equivalent units of **weight** in the standard system:
>
> 5,000 lb. ◯ 3 tn.
> Since 1 ton = 2,000 pounds, 3 tons would equal 6,000 pounds;
> 5,000 lb. < 3 tn.
>
> 1 pound (lb.) = 16 ounces (oz.)
>   1 ton (tn.) = 2,000 pounds (lb.)
>
> To change to a smaller unit, multiply.
> To change to a larger unit, divide.

Would you choose ounces, pounds, or tons to weigh the following?

A. a ship _____   a volleyball _____

B. an apple _____   a car _____

C. an adult _____   a paper clip _____

D. a bookcase _____   an elephant _____

Study the equivalents and the example above. Then, write >, <, or = to compare weights.

E.   2 lb. ◯ 40 oz.   64 oz. ◯ 4 lb

F.   4 lb. 18 oz. ◯ 5 lb.   4,002 lb. ◯ 2 tn. 34 oz.

G.   5 tn. ◯ 10,000 lb.   30 lb. ◯ 500 oz.

H.   6,000 lb. ◯ 3 tn.   3 lb. 16 oz. ◯ 4 lb.

I.   Fully clothed, Ray weighs 139 pounds.
         What will he weigh if he puts on a
         2 lb. 8 oz. jacket and a 9 oz. wool hat?   _____

Summer Bridge Math RB-904089

Weight in the Metric System

> A **gram** is a metric unit used to measure the weight of light objects, such as a piece of paper or a spoonful of sugar.
> A **kilogram** is used to weigh heavy objects like people or trucks.
>
> 1 kilogram (kg) = 1,000 grams (g)
> To change kilograms to grams multiply by 1,000. To change grams to kilograms, divide by 1,000.
>
> Since 1 kg = 1,000 g,
> 5 kg = 5,000 g.

Would you use grams (g) or kilograms (kg) to weigh the following?

A. an automobile _____   a letter _____   a piano _____

B. a dog _____   a feather _____   a textbook _____

Study the example above. Then, find each missing number.

C. 4 kg = _____ g   5,000 g = _____ kg

D. 6 kg = _____ g   6,500 g = _____ kg

E. 9,000 g = _____ kg   4.5 kg = _____ g

F. 20,000 g = _____ kg   7 kg = _____ g

G. 7,500 g = _____ kg   1.5 kg = _____ g

H. 12,000 g = _____ kg   11 kg = _____ g

I. A box of dimes weighs 300 grams. If each dime weighs 2 grams, how many dimes are in the box?

_____

Summer Bridge Math RB-904089

Time

> These are equivalent units of **time**:
>
> Since 1 week = 7 days,
> 4 weeks = 28 days.
>
> 1 year (yr.) = 12 months (mo.)
> 24 hours (hr.) = 1 day
> 7 days = 1 week
> 60 minutes (min.) = 1 hour. (hr.)

Study the equivalents above. Then, find each missing number.

A. 24 mo. = _____ yr.   5 weeks = _____ days   9 yr. = _____ mo.

B. 14 days = _____ weeks   8 hr. = _____ min.   49 days = _____ weeks

C. 120 min. = _____ hr.   60 mo. = _____ yr.   9 weeks = _____ days

D. 5 hr. = _____ min.   15 yr. = _____ mo.   40 hr. = _____ min.

E. 7 yr. = _____ mo.   6 weeks = _____ days   240 min. = _____ hr.

Solve each problem.

F. Gary spent 4 weeks biking for his vacation. How many days was he on vacation?

_____

G. Angela went on vacation for 28 days. How many weeks was she on vacation?

_____

H. Randy's flight was 480 minutes. How many hours did he spend flying?

_____

I. James kept track of the time he spent exercising. He walked on his treadmill for 45 minutes each day. How many hours and minutes did he spend walking after 14 days?

_____

Summer Bridge Math RB-904089

Identifying Fractions

A **fraction** tells about equal parts of a whole. The top number, called the **numerator**, tells how many parts are shaded. The bottom number, called the **denominator**, tells how many parts in all.

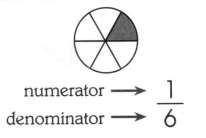

numerator ⟶ $\dfrac{1}{6}$
denominator ⟶

Study the example above. Then, write each fraction.

A.

B.

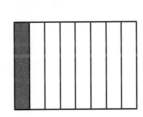

C.

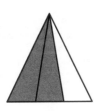

D.

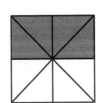

E.

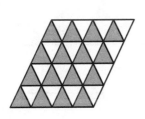

F.

G.

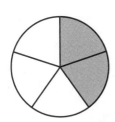

H.

Summer Bridge Math RB-904089

Fractions as Words

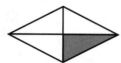

$\frac{1}{4}$ of the rectangle is shaded.

$\frac{1}{4}$ is read as one-fourth.

$\frac{2}{3}$ of the circle is <u>not</u> shaded.

$\frac{2}{3}$ is read as two-thirds.

Study the examples above. Then, write each word as a fraction.

A.   three-fifths   _____   three-fourths   _____

B.   four-ninths   _____   one-fourth   _____

C.   one-third   _____   six-twelfths   _____

D.   two-eighths   _____   four-tenths   _____

E.   four-fifths   _____   five-elevenths   _____

F.   one-half   _____   seven-eighths   _____

Write the words for each given fraction.

G. $\frac{1}{3}$ _____ $\frac{2}{3}$ _____

H. $\frac{1}{2}$ _____ $\frac{1}{8}$ _____

I. $\frac{3}{8}$ _____ $\frac{4}{11}$ _____

J. $\frac{2}{5}$ _____ $\frac{5}{3}$ _____

K. $\frac{5}{7}$ _____ $\frac{5}{9}$ _____

L. $\frac{4}{3}$ _____ $\frac{9}{2}$ _____

Summer Bridge Math RB-904089

Simplifying Fractions

$\frac{4}{8} = \frac{4 \div 4}{8 \div 4}$

$= \frac{1}{2}$

A fraction is **simplified** when 1 is the only number that divides into both the numerator and the denominator. To simplify, divide the numerator and denominator by the same number.

$\frac{12}{18} = \frac{12 \div 2}{18 \div 2}$

$= \frac{6}{9}$

$\frac{6}{9}$ is not simplified.

$\frac{6}{9} = \frac{6 \div 3}{9 \div 3}$

$= \frac{2}{3}$

Study the examples above. Then, simplify each fraction.

A. $\frac{4}{8} =$ _____ $\frac{4}{10} =$ _____ $\frac{8}{24} =$ _____

B. $\frac{4}{6} =$ _____ $\frac{5}{15} =$ _____ $\frac{6}{10} =$ _____

C. $\frac{6}{8} =$ _____ $\frac{2}{24} =$ _____ $\frac{8}{12} =$ _____

D. $\frac{3}{9} =$ _____ $\frac{6}{24} =$ _____ $\frac{10}{12} =$ _____

E. $\frac{6}{12} =$ _____ $\frac{5}{20} =$ _____ $\frac{14}{14} =$ _____

Finding Equivalent Fractions

Equivalent fractions are fractions that are equal. To find equivalent fractions, multiply any fraction by 1 or by a fraction equal to 1. Think about it as multiplying the numerator and the denominator by the same number.

$$\frac{1}{2} = \qquad \frac{2}{4} =$$

$$\frac{3}{6} = \qquad \frac{4}{8} =$$

$$\frac{1}{2} \times \frac{2}{2} = \frac{2}{4} \qquad \frac{1}{2} \times \frac{3}{3} = \frac{3}{6} \qquad \frac{1}{2} \times \frac{4}{4} = \frac{4}{8}$$

Study the examples above. Then, cross out each fraction that is not equivalent to the first fraction.

A. $\quad \dfrac{1}{3} = \dfrac{2}{6} \quad \dfrac{3}{9} \quad \dfrac{4}{8} \quad \dfrac{5}{15} \quad \dfrac{6}{18}$ $\qquad \dfrac{1}{4} = \dfrac{2}{8} \quad \dfrac{3}{6} \quad \dfrac{4}{16} \quad \dfrac{5}{20} \quad \dfrac{6}{24}$

B. $\quad \dfrac{1}{5} = \dfrac{2}{6} \quad \dfrac{2}{10} \quad \dfrac{3}{15} \quad \dfrac{4}{20} \quad \dfrac{5}{25}$ $\qquad \dfrac{2}{3} = \dfrac{4}{6} \quad \dfrac{6}{9} \quad \dfrac{8}{16} \quad \dfrac{10}{15} \quad \dfrac{12}{18}$

Fill in the missing number.

C. $\quad \dfrac{1}{4} = \dfrac{3}{\boxed{}}$ $\qquad\qquad \dfrac{2}{\boxed{}} = \dfrac{4}{6}$ $\qquad\qquad \dfrac{5}{8} = \dfrac{\boxed{}}{16}$

D. $\quad \dfrac{3}{4} = \dfrac{9}{\boxed{}}$ $\qquad\qquad \dfrac{\boxed{}}{6} = \dfrac{2}{12}$ $\qquad\qquad \dfrac{2}{3} = \dfrac{\boxed{}}{9}$

Summer Bridge Math RB-904089

The **least common denominator (LCD)** for two fractions is the least common multiple of the denominators.

Example: Find the LCD of $\frac{2}{3}$ and $\frac{3}{4}$. Rewrite each fraction using the LCD.

1. List the multiples of each denominator.
   $3 = 3, 6, 9, \textcircled{12}, 15, 18, 21, 24, \ldots$
   $4 = 4, 8, \textcircled{12}, 16, 20, 24, \ldots$

2. The LCD = 12.

$$\frac{2}{3} = \frac{}{12} \longleftarrow \text{The LCD of 3 and 4} \qquad \frac{3}{4} = \frac{}{12} \longleftarrow \text{The LCD of 3 and 4}$$

$$\frac{2}{3} = \frac{2 \times 4}{3 \times 4} = \frac{8}{12} \qquad\qquad \frac{3}{4} = \frac{3 \times 3}{4 \times 3} = \frac{9}{12}$$

$$\frac{2}{3} = \mathbf{\frac{8}{12}} \qquad\qquad\qquad \frac{3}{4} = \mathbf{\frac{9}{12}}$$

Study the example above. Then, find the LCD of each pair of fractions. Rewrite each fraction using the new common denominator.

A. $\frac{2}{3}$, $\frac{4}{5}$

B. $\frac{1}{2}$, $\frac{1}{3}$

C. $\frac{2}{5}$, $\frac{1}{2}$

D. $\frac{3}{4}$, $\frac{1}{5}$

E. $\frac{1}{7}$, $\frac{2}{3}$

F. $\frac{6}{7}$, $\frac{1}{3}$

G. $\frac{1}{2}$, $\frac{3}{5}$

H. $\frac{4}{7}$, $\frac{1}{2}$

I. $\frac{2}{3}$, $\frac{5}{8}$

    Summer Bridge Math RB-904089

Fractions Equal to and Greater Than One

This fraction shows $\frac{5}{3}$. Five-thirds is called an **improper fraction** because the numerator is larger than the denominator. Three-thirds ($\frac{3}{3}$) equals 1 whole, so $\frac{5}{3}$ equals 1 whole and $\frac{2}{3}$. One and two-thirds ($1\frac{2}{3}$) is called a **mixed number**.

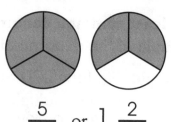

$$\frac{5}{3} \quad \text{or} \quad 1\frac{2}{3}$$

Study the example above. Then, write each group as an improper fraction and as a mixed number.

A.

——— or ———

B.

——— or ———

C.

——— or ———

D.

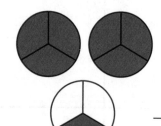

——— or ———

E.

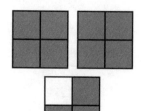

——— or ———

F.

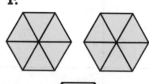

——— or ———

To change an **improper fraction** to a mixed number, divide the numerator by the denominator and place the remainder as the numerator.

$14 \div 3 = 4$ with 2 left over. So $\frac{14}{3}$ can be renamed $4\frac{2}{3}$.

$$\frac{14}{3} = 4\frac{2}{3}$$

Study the example above. Then, rewrite each fraction as a mixed number.

A. $\frac{5}{4} = $ _____ $\frac{10}{3} = $ _____ $\frac{9}{8} = $ _____ $\frac{8}{3} = $ _____

B. $\frac{5}{2} = $ _____ $\frac{7}{4} = $ _____ $\frac{9}{3} = $ _____ $\frac{11}{10} = $ _____

C. $\frac{10}{7} = $ _____ $\frac{19}{8} = $ _____ $\frac{9}{5} = $ _____ $\frac{31}{10} = $ _____

D. $\frac{23}{10} = $ _____ $\frac{17}{8} = $ _____ $\frac{13}{3} = $ _____ $\frac{25}{12} = $ _____

E. $\frac{28}{9} = $ _____ $\frac{9}{4} = $ _____ $\frac{13}{6} = $ _____ $\frac{76}{25} = $ _____

Simplifying Mixed Numbers

$2\dfrac{5}{15} = 2 + \dfrac{5}{15}$

$= 2 + \dfrac{5 \div 5}{15 \div 5}$

$= 2 + \dfrac{1}{3}$

$= \mathbf{2\dfrac{1}{3}}$

When simplifying mixed numbers, simplify the fraction.

$3\dfrac{9}{6} = 3 + \dfrac{9}{6}$

$= 3 + \dfrac{9 \div 3}{6 \div 3}$

$= 3 + \dfrac{3}{2}$

Change to a mixed number.

$= 3 + 1\dfrac{1}{2}$

$= 3 + 1 + \dfrac{1}{2} = \mathbf{4\dfrac{1}{2}}$

Study the examples above. Then, simplify.

A. $2\dfrac{2}{4} = $ _____ $3\dfrac{5}{15} = $ _____ $2\dfrac{12}{16} = $ _____

B. $1\dfrac{6}{9} = $ _____ $2\dfrac{9}{2} = $ _____ $6\dfrac{3}{3} = $ _____

C. $2\dfrac{5}{20} = $ _____ $4\dfrac{7}{21} = $ _____ $5\dfrac{9}{6} = $ _____

D. $4\dfrac{9}{3} = $ _____ $5\dfrac{3}{12} = $ _____ $2\dfrac{3}{2} = $ _____

Summer Bridge Math RB-904089

Adding Fractions

When adding fractions with unlike denominators:

$$\frac{2}{3} \longrightarrow \frac{2 \times 4}{3 \times 4} \longrightarrow \frac{8}{12}$$

$$+ \; \frac{1}{4} \longrightarrow \frac{1 \times 3}{4 \times 3} \longrightarrow \frac{3}{12}$$

$$\frac{11}{12}$$

1. Find the least common denominator (LCD).
2. Rewrite each fraction using the LCD.
3. Add.
4. Simplify, if possible.

$$\frac{5}{6} \longrightarrow \frac{5 \times 5}{6 \times 5} \longrightarrow \frac{25}{30}$$

$$+ \; \frac{2}{5} \longrightarrow \frac{2 \times 6}{5 \times 6} \longrightarrow \frac{12}{30}$$

$$\frac{37}{30}$$

$$= 1\frac{7}{30}$$

Study the examples above. Then, add. Simplify, if possible.

A.

$$\frac{2}{5}$$
$$+ \; \frac{1}{3}$$

$$\frac{3}{8}$$
$$+ \; \frac{1}{3}$$

$$\frac{1}{2}$$
$$+ \; \frac{1}{3}$$

$$\frac{3}{4}$$
$$+ \; \frac{3}{5}$$

B.

$$\frac{5}{6}$$
$$+ \; \frac{2}{5}$$

$$\frac{2}{7}$$
$$+ \; \frac{2}{3}$$

$$\frac{3}{10}$$
$$+ \; \frac{1}{3}$$

$$\frac{5}{9}$$
$$+ \; \frac{1}{2}$$

C.

$$\frac{3}{4}$$
$$+ \; \frac{1}{7}$$

$$\frac{1}{3}$$
$$+ \; \frac{5}{8}$$

$$\frac{1}{3}$$
$$+ \; \frac{3}{4}$$

$$\frac{7}{10}$$
$$+ \; \frac{2}{3}$$

© Rainbow Bridge Publishing

Summer Bridge Math RB-904089

Subtracting Fractions

To subtract a fraction from a whole number:

$$3 \longrightarrow 2\frac{4}{4}$$
$$-\frac{1}{4} \longrightarrow \frac{1}{4}$$
$$\overline{2\frac{3}{4}}$$

1. Rewrite the whole number as an equivalent fraction using the LCD.
2. Subtract.

$$2 \longrightarrow 1\frac{6}{6}$$
$$-\frac{5}{6} \longrightarrow \frac{5}{6}$$
$$\overline{1\frac{1}{6}}$$

Study the examples above. Then, subtract.

A.

$$5 \qquad\qquad 3 \qquad\qquad 6 \qquad\qquad 4$$
$$-\frac{7}{8} \qquad\quad -\frac{1}{3} \qquad\quad -\frac{7}{9} \qquad\quad -\frac{2}{5}$$

B.

$$8 \qquad\qquad 5 \qquad\qquad 12 \qquad\qquad 9$$
$$-\frac{4}{5} \qquad\quad -\frac{4}{9} \qquad\quad -\frac{3}{11} \qquad\quad -\frac{8}{9}$$

C.

$$7 \qquad\qquad 10 \qquad\qquad 12 \qquad\qquad 8$$
$$-\frac{1}{3} \qquad\quad -\frac{1}{5} \qquad\quad -\frac{7}{10} \qquad\quad -\frac{5}{6}$$

Adding Mixed Numbers

To add mixed numbers:

$$3\frac{2}{6}$$
$$+\ 2\frac{1}{6}$$
$$\overline{5\frac{3}{6}} = \mathbf{5\frac{1}{2}}$$

1. Add the fractions.
2. Add the whole numbers.
3. Simplify, if possible.

$$2\frac{5}{12}$$
$$+\ 1\frac{11}{12}$$
$$\overline{3\frac{16}{12}} = 3 + 1 + \frac{4}{12} = \mathbf{4\frac{1}{3}}$$

Study the examples above. Then, add. Simplify, if possible.

A.

$$3\frac{1}{3}$$
$$+\ 2\frac{1}{3}$$

$$4\frac{2}{5}$$
$$+\ \frac{1}{5}$$

$$3\frac{3}{8}$$
$$+\ 2\frac{5}{8}$$

$$7\frac{3}{4}$$
$$+\ 5\frac{3}{4}$$

B.

$$2\frac{4}{5}$$
$$+\ 3\frac{2}{5}$$

$$13\frac{2}{8}$$
$$+\ \frac{7}{8}$$

$$1\frac{3}{4}$$
$$+\ 2\frac{3}{4}$$

$$4\frac{1}{7}$$
$$+\ 2\frac{2}{7}$$

C.

$$10\frac{2}{9}$$
$$+\ 2\frac{7}{9}$$

$$3\frac{5}{6}$$
$$+\ 2\frac{3}{6}$$

$$2\frac{7}{10}$$
$$+\ 1\frac{4}{10}$$

$$3\frac{3}{5}$$
$$+\ 1\frac{1}{5}$$

Summer Bridge Math RB-904089

Subtracting Mixed Numbers

Rewrite $3\frac{1}{4}$ so that you can subtract.

$$3\frac{1}{4} = 2 + 1\frac{1}{4} = 2\frac{5}{4}$$

$$-\ 1\frac{3}{4} \longrightarrow 1\frac{3}{4}$$

$$1\frac{2}{4} = \mathbf{1\frac{1}{2}}$$

Rewrite $3\frac{2}{9}$ so that you can subtract.

$$6\frac{2}{9} = 5 + 1\frac{2}{9} = 5\frac{11}{9}$$

$$-\ 5\frac{4}{9} \longrightarrow 5\frac{4}{9}$$

$$\frac{7}{9}$$

Study the examples above. Then, subtract. Simplify, if possible.

A.

$3\frac{3}{7}$ $\quad$ $5\frac{1}{3}$ $\quad$ $4\frac{1}{6}$ $\quad$ $8\frac{3}{8}$

$-\ 1\frac{5}{7}$ $\quad$ $-\ 2\frac{2}{3}$ $\quad$ $-\ 3\frac{5}{6}$ $\quad$ $-\ 2\frac{5}{8}$

B.

$6\frac{1}{5}$ $\quad$ $4\frac{3}{10}$ $\quad$ $8\frac{2}{5}$ $\quad$ $10\frac{5}{12}$

$-\ 3\frac{3}{5}$ $\quad$ $-\ 3\frac{7}{10}$ $\quad$ $-\ 5\frac{4}{5}$ $\quad$ $-\ 7\frac{7}{12}$

C.

$3\frac{1}{8}$ $\quad$ $6\frac{4}{9}$ $\quad$ $12\frac{5}{12}$ $\quad$ $9\frac{1}{4}$

$-\ 2\frac{5}{8}$ $\quad$ $-\ 5\frac{7}{9}$ $\quad$ $-\ 10\frac{7}{12}$ $\quad$ $-\ 3\frac{3}{4}$

Summer Bridge Math RB-904089 $\qquad$

Multiplying Fractions

When multiplying $\dfrac{1}{2}$ x $\dfrac{1}{4}$:

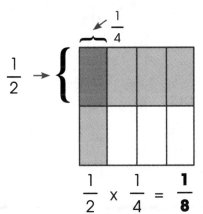

$$\dfrac{1}{2} \times \dfrac{1}{4} = \dfrac{1}{8}$$

1. Multiply the numerators.
2. Multiply the denominators.
3. Simplify, if possible.

$$\dfrac{1}{2} \times \dfrac{1}{4} = \dfrac{1 \times 1}{2 \times 4} = \dfrac{1}{8}$$

$$\dfrac{3}{4} \times \dfrac{1}{7} = \dfrac{1 \times 3}{4 \times 7} = \dfrac{3}{28}$$

Study the examples above. Then, multiply. Simplify, if possible.

A. $\dfrac{1}{2} \times \dfrac{3}{4}$ ____ $\dfrac{2}{3} \times \dfrac{1}{5}$ ____ $\dfrac{2}{5} \times \dfrac{1}{3}$ ____ $\dfrac{5}{6} \times \dfrac{1}{2}$ ____ $\dfrac{1}{4} \times \dfrac{3}{8}$ ____

B. $\dfrac{5}{12} \times \dfrac{1}{2}$ ____ $\dfrac{1}{2} \times \dfrac{5}{7}$ ____ $\dfrac{1}{3} \times \dfrac{1}{4}$ ____ $\dfrac{1}{5} \times \dfrac{2}{5}$ ____ $\dfrac{3}{5} \times \dfrac{1}{2}$ ____

C. $\dfrac{3}{4} \times \dfrac{1}{8}$ ____ $\dfrac{2}{5} \times \dfrac{3}{5}$ ____ $\dfrac{1}{2} \times \dfrac{1}{2}$ ____ $\dfrac{2}{3} \times \dfrac{2}{3}$ ____ $\dfrac{3}{8} \times \dfrac{1}{2}$ ____

D. $\dfrac{5}{7} \times \dfrac{1}{3}$ ____ $\dfrac{1}{2} \times \dfrac{3}{7}$ ____ $\dfrac{5}{8} \times \dfrac{1}{3}$ ____ $\dfrac{5}{6} \times \dfrac{1}{3}$ ____ $\dfrac{3}{5} \times \dfrac{1}{7}$ ____

Multiplying Fractions by Whole Numbers

When multiplying a whole number and a fraction:

$$8 \times \frac{3}{8} = \frac{8 \times 3}{1 \times 8}$$

$$= \frac{8 \times 3}{1 \times 8}$$

$$= \frac{24}{8}$$

$$= \mathbf{3}$$

1. Rewrite the whole number as a fraction (write a denominator of 1).
2. Multiply the numerators.
3. Multiply the denominators.
4. Simplify, if possible.

$$\frac{3}{4} \times 6 = \frac{3 \times 6}{4 \times 1}$$

$$= \frac{3 \times 6}{4 \times 1}$$

$$= \frac{18}{4}$$

$$= 4\frac{2}{4} = \mathbf{4\frac{1}{2}}$$

Study the examples above. Then, multiply. Simplify, if possible.

A. $3 \times \dfrac{2}{3} =$ _____ $\dfrac{4}{5} \times 2 =$ _____ $1 \times \dfrac{6}{7} =$ _____ $2 \times \dfrac{4}{7} =$ _____

B. $\dfrac{2}{5} \times 6 =$ _____ $3 \times \dfrac{3}{10} =$ _____ $9 \times \dfrac{3}{4} =$ _____ $6 \times \dfrac{3}{10} =$ _____

C. $8 \times \dfrac{1}{6} =$ _____ $2 \times \dfrac{6}{7} =$ _____ $6 \times \dfrac{1}{4} =$ _____ $\dfrac{3}{8} \times 4 =$ _____

D. $\dfrac{3}{10} \times 5 =$ _____ $5 \times \dfrac{2}{9} =$ _____ $\dfrac{3}{7} \times 2 =$ _____ $\dfrac{2}{3} \times 4 =$ _____

Multiplying Mixed Numbers

When multiplying mixed numbers:

$$3\frac{3}{4} \times 3\frac{3}{4} = \frac{15}{4} \times \frac{15}{4}$$

$$= \frac{15}{4} \times \frac{15}{4}$$

$$= \frac{225}{16}$$

$$= 14\frac{1}{16}$$

1. Rewrite the numbers as improper fractions.
2. Multiply the numerators.
3. Multiply the denominators.
4. Simplify, if possible.

$$1\frac{1}{3} \times 2\frac{1}{8} = \frac{4}{3} \times \frac{17}{8}$$

$$= \frac{4}{3} \times \frac{17}{8}$$

$$= \frac{68}{24}$$

$$= 2\frac{20}{24} = 2\frac{5}{6}$$

Study the examples above. Then, multiply. Simplify, if possible.

A. $3\frac{3}{4} \times 2\frac{2}{3} =$ _____ $1\frac{1}{4} \times 2\frac{1}{2} =$ _____ $2\frac{1}{5} \times 2\frac{1}{4} =$ _____

B. $1\frac{3}{5} \times 1\frac{2}{5} =$ _____ $2\frac{1}{2} \times 3\frac{1}{3} =$ _____ $4\frac{1}{2} \times 1\frac{2}{3} =$ _____

C. $2\frac{3}{8} \times 2\frac{1}{3} =$ _____ $1\frac{4}{5} \times 1\frac{1}{4} =$ _____ $1\frac{3}{7} \times 1\frac{3}{8} =$ _____

D. $4\frac{1}{2} \times 1\frac{2}{5} =$ _____ $3\frac{2}{3} \times 1\frac{1}{2} =$ _____ $4\frac{1}{2} \times 1\frac{1}{2} =$ _____

Summer Bridge Math RB-904089

Visualizing Decimals

$\frac{5}{10}$ or 0.5

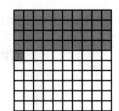

$\frac{41}{100}$ or 0.41

Study the examples above. Then, write the fraction and the decimal for each figure.

	Fraction	Decimal

A. 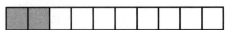   _____   _____

B.    _____   _____

C.   _____   _____

D.   _____   _____

E. 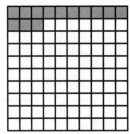   _____   _____

F. 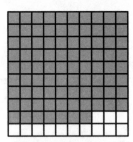   _____   _____

G. 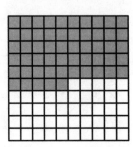   _____   _____

58

Place Value

You should already know the place value names for numbers larger than 0. There are also names for place values after the decimal.

thousands	hundreds	tens	ones		tenths	hundredths	thousandths
1	2	4	5	.	1	7	6

Decimal	Read As	Equivalent Fraction
0.1	one-tenth	$\frac{1}{10}$
0.7	seven-tenths	$\frac{7}{10}$
0.23	twenty-three hundredths	$\frac{23}{100}$
0.05	five-hundredths	$\frac{5}{100}$
0.783	seven hundred eighty-three thousandths	$\frac{783}{1000}$
0.045	forty-five thousandths	$\frac{45}{1000}$
2.6	two and six-tenths	$2\frac{6}{10}$
15.01	fifteen and one-hundredth	$15\frac{1}{100}$

Study the place values above. Then, complete the chart below.

	Decimal	Read As	Equivalent Fraction
A.	0.3	three-tenths	_____
B.	1.12	_____	_____
C.	_____	two hundred twenty-one thousandths	_____
D.	_____	_____	$\frac{53}{100}$
E.	0.871	_____	_____
F.	_____	_____	$2\frac{1}{100}$

Tenths and Hundredths

> **Decimals** can be written as words as well as numbers.
>
> four-tenths = 0.4
> three-hundredths = 0.03
> 1.8 = one and eight-tenths
> 0.56 = fifty-six hundredths

Study the examples above. Then, write a decimal for each problem.

A. one-tenth   seven-tenths   six-hundredths

_____   _____   _____

B. eleven-hundredths   two and two-tenths   nine-tenths

_____   _____   _____

C. one and five-hundredths   five and six-tenths   five and six-hundredths

_____   _____   _____

D. eighty-six hundredths   nineteen hundredths   twelve-hundredths

_____   _____   _____

Write each decimal in words.

E. 0.8 _____

F. 0.08 _____

G. 3.05 _____

H. 0.53 _____

I. 5.53 _____

J. 1.14 _____

K. 0.9 _____

L. 0.01 _____

M. 3.28 _____

Summer Bridge Math RB-904089

Comparing Decimals

Comparing decimals is similar to comparing whole numbers.
1. Line up the numbers by place value.
2. Compare the digits left to right.

$$0.08 \bigcirc 0.8 \qquad\qquad 11.13 \bigcirc 11.03$$

1. Line up: 0.08   11.13
              0.8   11.03
2. Compare.

After the decimal point, there are   The 11s before the decimal point
a 0 and an 8. Eight is bigger than 0,   are the same. After the decimal
so 0.8 is bigger.   point, is 1 or 0 bigger? One is.
0.08 < 0.8   11.13 > 11.03

Study the examples above. Then, use >, <, or = to compare each decimal.

A.   0.007 $\bigcirc$ 0.07   0.08 $\bigcirc$ 0.8

B.   2.159 $\bigcirc$ 2.259   101.05 $\bigcirc$ 101.005

C.   10.05 $\bigcirc$ 10.005   9.50 $\bigcirc$ 7.05

D.   0.99 $\bigcirc$ .009   214.01 $\bigcirc$ 214.001

E.   30.249 $\bigcirc$ 30.429   9.008 $\bigcirc$ 9.08

F.   0.004 $\bigcirc$ 4.00   614.05 $\bigcirc$ 614.05

G.   6.041 $\bigcirc$ 6.401   8.26 $\bigcirc$ 8.026

H.   92.001 $\bigcirc$ 92.001   43.014 $\bigcirc$ 43.104

Summer Bridge Math RB-904089

Equivalent Fractions and Decimals

All numbers can be written as decimals, as words, or as fractions.

$$0.95 = 95 \text{ hundredths} = \frac{95}{100} \qquad \frac{7}{10} = 7 \text{ tenths} = 0.7$$
$$0.1 = 1 \text{ tenth} = \frac{1}{10} \qquad \frac{15}{100} = 15 \text{ hundredths} = 0.15$$

Study the examples above. Then, write a decimal for each fraction.

A. $\frac{5}{10}$ = _____ $\frac{3}{100}$ = _____ $\frac{45}{100}$ = _____

B. $\frac{9}{10}$ = _____ $\frac{25}{100}$ = _____ $\frac{60}{100}$ = _____

C. $\frac{76}{100}$ = _____ $\frac{2}{10}$ = _____ $\frac{4}{10}$ = _____

Write a fraction for each decimal.

D.   0.67 = _____   0.3 = _____   0.81 = _____

E.   0.73 = _____   0.55 = _____   0.6 = _____

F.   0.05 = _____   0.33 = _____   0.8 = _____

Use >, <, or = to compare each pair of numbers.

G. $\frac{2}{10}$ ◯ 0.5   0.51 ◯ $\frac{55}{100}$ 0.39 ◯ $\frac{4}{10}$

Summer Bridge Math RB-904089

Decimals and Mixed Numbers

$3\frac{5}{10} = 3.5$, since $\frac{5}{10} = .5$ $6.14 =$ six and fourteen-hundredths

Study the examples above and the chart on page 59. Then, write a decimal for each problem below.

A. $2\frac{9}{10} = $ —————— $12\frac{19}{100} = $ ——————

B.   five and ten-hundredths = ————   three and two-tenths = ————

C. $6\frac{42}{100} = $ ———— $9\frac{6}{10} = $ ————

D.   twelve and twelve-hundredths = ————   one and fifty-one hundredths = ————

Write each decimal or mixed number in words.

E. $9.1 = $ _____ $0.07 = $ _____

F. $0.4 = $ _____ $5.99 = $ _____

G. $10.01 = $ _____ $0.32 = $ _____

H. $5\frac{6}{10} = $ _____ $11\frac{11}{100} = $ _____

     Summer Bridge Math RB-904089

Mixed Practice

Study the examples on pages 58–62. Then, write each fraction as a decimal.

A. $4\frac{4}{10}$ _____ $\frac{23}{100}$ _____

B. $1\frac{3}{100}$ _____ $\frac{5}{10}$ _____

C. $\frac{548}{1000}$ _____ $2\frac{53}{100}$ _____

D. $53\frac{17}{100}$ _____ $16\frac{303}{1000}$ _____

E. $\frac{91}{1000}$ _____ $91\frac{3}{10}$ _____

Write each decimal as a mixed number or a fraction.

F. 2.87 _____   0.983 _____

G. 14.5 _____   287.69 _____

H. 1.752 _____   0.7 _____

I. 0.06 _____   10.054 _____

J. 81.2 _____   0.157 _____

Polygons

Some **polygons** have more than one classification. These are the general names of polygons, named for the number of sides.

triangle   quadrilateral   pentagon   hexagon   heptagon   octagon
3 sides   4 sides   5 sides   6 sides   7 sides   8 sides

 A square is a quadrilateral because it has 4 sides.

Study the shapes above. Then, write the general name for each figure.

A.

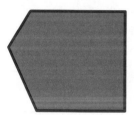 _____

B.

 _____ 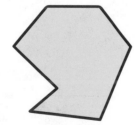 _____

C.

 _____  _____

© Rainbow Bridge Publishing

Quadrilaterals

A **quadrilateral** has 4 sides.

A **trapezoid** is a quadrilateral that has exactly 1 pair of parallel sides.

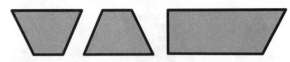

A **parallelogram** is a quadrilateral that has 2 pairs of parallel sides.

A **rectangle** is a parallelogram that has 4 right angles.

A **square** is a rectangle that has 4 equal sides.

Study the examples above. Then, classify the following quadrilaterals as (a.) quadrilateral, (b.) trapezoid, (c.) parallelogram, (d.) rectangle, or (e.) square. There may be more than 1 answer.

A.

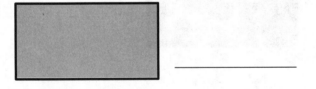 _____

 _____

B.

 _____

  _____

C.

 _____

  _____

Summer Bridge Math RB-904089

Three-Dimensional Objects

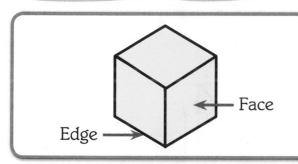

A cube has 6 faces (sides). A **face** is a flat surface.

Face

A cube has 12 edges. An **edge** is a line segment where two faces meet.

Edge

Study the example above. Then, write the number of faces and edges for each figure.

	Faces	Edges

A.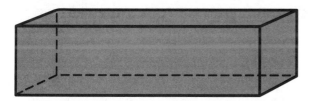

_____   _____

B.

_____   _____

C.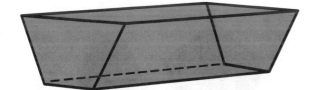

_____   _____

D.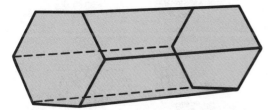

_____   _____

E.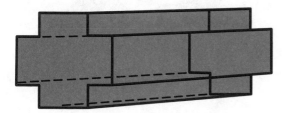

_____   _____

Summer Bridge Math RB-904089

Congruent and Similar

Congruent polygons have equal lengths and angles.
Similar polygons have equal angles.

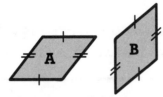 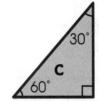

Parallelograms A and B are **congruent**.   Triangles C and D are **similar** triangles.

Study the example above. Then, classify each pair as (c) congruent or (s) similar.

A.  _____   _____

B.  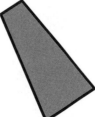 _____    _____

C.    _____   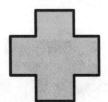 _____

Summer Bridge Math RB-904089

Lines of Symmetry

If a figure can be folded along a line so that the 2 halves match perfectly, then the line is a **line of symmetry**. A square has 4 lines of symmetry.

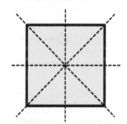

Study the example above. Then, draw the lines of symmetry for each object. Write the number of lines of symmetry.

A.

 Lines: _____

 Lines: _____

 Lines: _____

B.

 Lines: _____

 Lines: _____

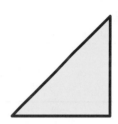 Lines: _____

C.

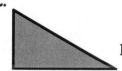 Lines: _____

 Lines: _____

 Lines: _____

D.

 Lines: _____

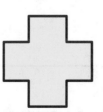 Lines: _____

 Lines: _____

Summer Bridge Math RB-904089

Basic Figures

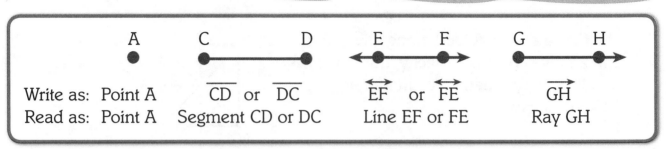

	A	C D	E F	G H
Write as:	Point A	$\overline{CD}$ or $\overline{DC}$	$\overleftrightarrow{EF}$ or $\overleftrightarrow{FE}$	$\overrightarrow{GH}$
Read as:	Point A	Segment CD or DC	Line EF or FE	Ray GH

Study the examples above. Then, name each figure.

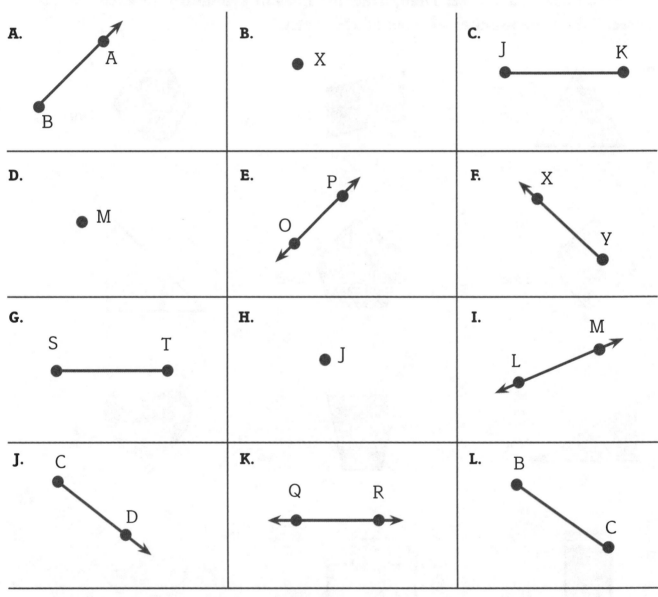

A.

B. • X

C. J ———— K

D. • M

E. O P

F. X Y

G. S ———— T

H. • J

I. L M

J. C D

K. Q R

L. B C

M. Name the line segments. Name the rays.

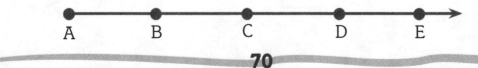

A   B   C   D   E

Summer Bridge Math RB-904089

Angles

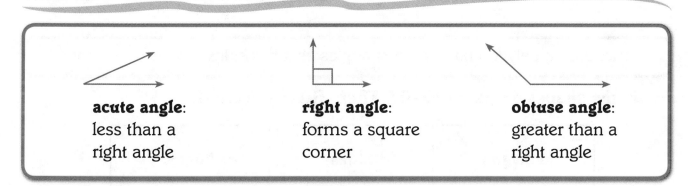

acute angle: less than a right angle

right angle: forms a square corner

obtuse angle: greater than a right angle

Classify each angle as acute, right, or obtuse.

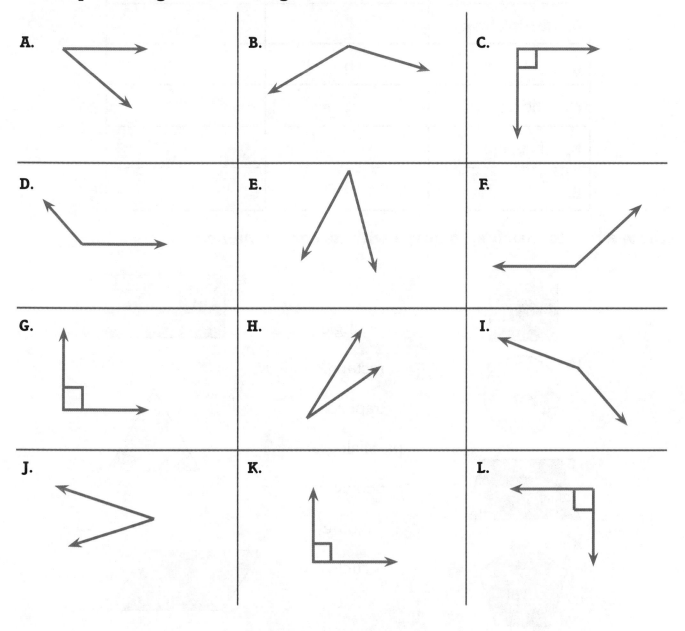

A.

B.

C.

D.

E.

F.

G.

H.

I.

J.

K.

L.

Summer Bridge Math RB-904089

Attributes of Shapes

> Remember, a polygon has as many angles as it has sides.

Study the shapes on pages 65–67. Then, fill in the chart.

Polygon	Sides	Angles
triangle	3	3
A. quadrilateral		
B.	5	
C. hexagon		6
D. heptagon		
E.	8	

Draw a line to match each shape with its correct name.

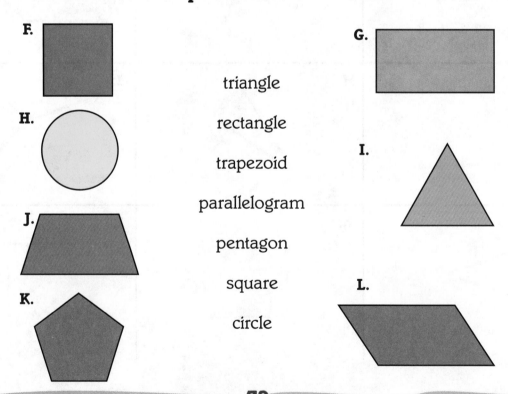

triangle

rectangle

trapezoid

parallelogram

pentagon

square

circle

Perimeter

The **perimeter** is the distance around a figure. To find the perimeter of a figure, add the lengths of all of the sides of the figure.

9 in.

3 in.

9 + 9 + 3 + 3 = 24 in.

Study the example above. Then, find the perimeter of each shape.

A.

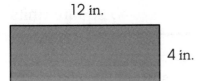

12 in.

4 in.

B.

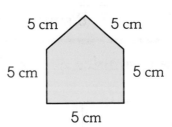

5 cm   5 cm

5 cm   5 cm

5 cm

C.

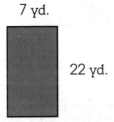

7 yd.

22 yd.

D.

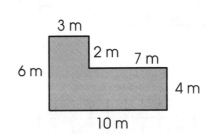

3 m

2 m   7 m

6 m

4 m

10 m

E.

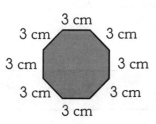

3 cm

3 cm   3 cm

3 cm   3 cm

3 cm   3 cm

3 cm

F.

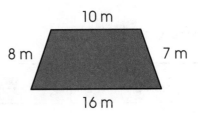

10 m

8 m   7 m

16 m

G.

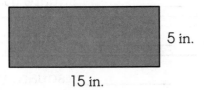

5 in.

15 in.

H.

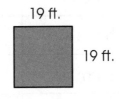

19 ft.

19 ft.

Summer Bridge Math RB-904089

Area

The **area** of a rectangle is equal to its length times its width.

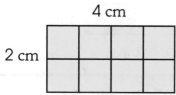

length
x width
area

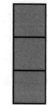

Area =   4
       x 2
       8 square cm

Area =   3
       x 1
       3 square units

Study the examples above. Then, find each area.

A.

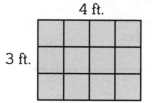

4 ft.

3 ft.

_____ square feet

5 m

5 m

_____ square meters

B.

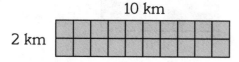

10 km

2 km

_____ square kilometers

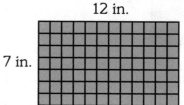

12 in.

7 in.

_____ square inches

Fill in the blanks.

	Length	Width	Area
C.	3 feet	6 feet	_____ square feet
D.	1 inch	4 inches	_____ square inches
E.	5 cm	6 cm	_____ square cm
F.	3 km	5 km	_____ square km
G.	4 mm	_____ mm	20 square mm

Tree Diagrams

Tammy and Debbie love potatoes. Their favorite restaurant gives a choice of a red potato or a brown potato. Also, it is served three different ways: mashed, baked, or as french fries. How many different choices are there? To find out, use a **tree diagram**.

Set up the choices for the red potato.

Then, set up the choices for the brown potato.

How many choices do they have altogether? There are 3 choices for the red potato and 3 choices for the brown. That makes a total of 6 different choices.

Study the example above. Then, use a separate sheet of paper to solve each problem. Use a tree diagram to help you.

A. David wants to buy a new bike. He has a choice of a mountain, road, or BMX bike. The store has each bike in red, blue, or purple. How many choices does David have in all?

B. Eva and four friends are at the school picnic together. They have decided to get something to eat. They have a choice between a hot dog or a hamburger. How many choices are there between all 5 friends?

C. Monica wants to buy a new binder for school. The store has $1\frac{1}{2}$" and 2" width binders. Each of these comes in red, blue, black, green, or brown. How many choices does she have in all?

D. Mark loves fruit! He is at the grocery store with his mom, and she says that she will buy for him apples or grapes. Each comes in red or green. How many choices does Mark have altogether?

E. Marlene's class divides into 5 lab groups for science. Each group must decide what type of plant they will grow for their science experiment. They can choose lima beans, string beans, yellow squash, corn, or watermelon. Among all 5 groups, how many choices can be made altogether?

Summer Bridge Math RB-904089

Graphs

Using a graph or a chart is a way to organize lots of information. The first graph is called a **bar graph**. The second graph is called a **line graph**.

Use the graphs to answer each question.

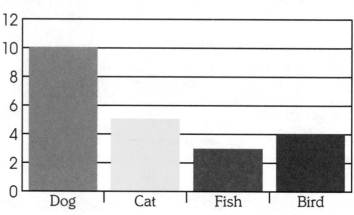

Favorite Pets in Kyle's Class

A. How many students favored

dogs? _____ cats? _____ fish? _____ birds? _____

B. Which pet was preferred the most? _____

C. Which pet was preferred the least? _____

D. How many more students liked cats than fish? _____

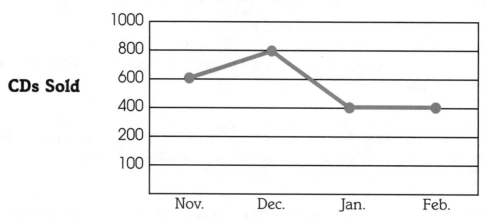

CDs Sold

E. In which month were the most CDs sold? _____

F. In which month were 600 CDs sold? _____

G. How many CDs were sold in all four months? _____

H. Why do you suppose there were more CDs sold in December than in other months?

_____

Summer Bridge Math RB-904089 © Rainbow Bridge Publishing

Reading a Schedule

Bus Number	Freeport	Austinville	Shadow	Vineville	Taylor
101	8:30 A.M.	10:30 A.M	2:00 P.M.	5:45 P.M.	9:15 P.M.
102	6:30 A.M.	8:30 A.M.	12:00 P.M.	3:45 P.M.	7:15 P.M.
103	11:30 A.M.	1:30 P.M.	5:00 P.M.	8:45 P.M.	12:15 A.M.
104	9:00 A.M.	11:00 A.M.	2:30 P.M.	6:15 P.M.	9:45 P.M.
105	9:15 A.M.	11:15 A.M.	2:45 P.M.	6:30 P.M.	10:00 P.M.
106	1:45 P.M.	3:45 P.M.	7:15 P.M.	10:45 P.M.	2:15 A.M.

Use the schedule of bus arrival times above to answer each question.

A. What time does bus number 103 arrive in Austinville? _____

B. What time does bus number 106 arrive in Vineville? _____

C. What time does bus number 102 arrive in Taylor? _____

D. What bus number arrives in Shadow at 2:00 P.M.? _____

E. How much later does bus 104 arrive after bus 102 in Shadow? _____

F. What time does bus number 106 arrive in Austinville? _____

G. What bus number arrives in Austinville at 11:00 A.M.? _____

H. Which bus or buses arrive at Taylor in the morning? _____

I. Which bus number arrives in Freeport the earliest? _____

J. Which bus arrives in Vineville at 10:45 P.M.? _____

77

Reading a Thermometer

Temperatures are measured in **Fahrenheit (F)** and **Celsius (C)**. 32 degrees Fahrenheit is equal to 0 degrees Celsius.

The thermometer to the right shows that the temperatue is 70°F. This means that the temperature outside is warm.

 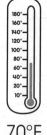

70°F

Study the example above. Then, write the temperature shown on each thermometer.

A.

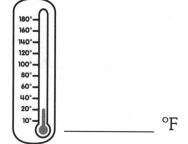

_____ °F   _____ °F   _____ °F

B.

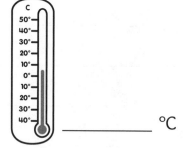   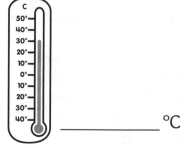

_____ °C   _____ °C   _____ °C

C.

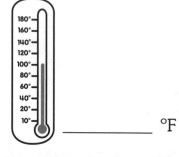   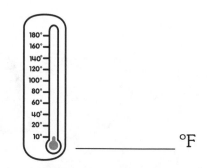

_____ °F   _____ °F   _____ °F

78

Finding Probabilities

Keshia has 12 pencils in her pencil box. One pencil is red, 3 are blue, 6 are yellow, and 2 are purple.

The probability that she would pull a blue pencil out of the box is $\frac{3}{12}$, because 3 of the 12 pencils are blue.

Probability is the chance or possibility that an event will happen. The probability of something happening can be written as a fraction.

$$\frac{3}{12}$$

The numerator tells the number of chances for a specific event (how many blue pencils).

The denominator tells the total number of possible things that could happen (how many total pencils).

- If the fraction that describes the probability is equal to 1, the event is **certain**.
- If the fraction is greater than another, the event is **more likely**.
- If the fraction is less than another, the event is **less likely**.
- If the fraction that describes the probability is 0, the event is **impossible**.

Study the example above. Then, find each probability.

Penny has 11 pencils in her pencil box. Two pencils are orange, 3 pencils are blue, 5 pencils are yellow, and 1 pencil is green.

A. What is the probability that Penny will pull out an orange pencil?

_____

B. What is the probability that Penny will pull out a green pencil?

_____

C. What is the probability that Penny will pull out a blue pencil?

_____

D. What is the probability that Penny will pull out a black pencil?

_____

E. What is the probability that Penny will pull out a yellow pencil?

_____

F. What color pencil is Penny most likely to pull out of her pencil box?

_____

Finding Probabilities (continued)

Use the probabilities from the problems on page 79 to describe whether the event is:

certain   likely   more likely   less likely   impossible

A. Pulling a green pencil from the box is _____ than pulling a blue pencil from the box.

B. Pulling a yellow pencil from the box is _____ than pulling a green pencil from the box.

C. Pulling a black pencil from the box is _____ .

D. Pulling an orange pencil from the box is _____ than pulling a blue pencil from the box.

E. Penny has a new box of 12 pencils, and 12 of the pencils are yellow. Pulling a yellow pencil from the box is _____ .

Use the scenario below to find each probability.

Each of the students in Ms. Evan's class took off his or her shoes and put them in a large bag. There were 24 shoes altogether. Ten shoes were sneakers, 2 were dress shoes, 4 were hiking shoes, and 8 were sandals.

F. What is the probability that Nicole will pull a sneaker out of the bag? _____

G. What is the probability that Colton will pull a dress shoe out of the bag? _____

H. What is the probability that Steven will pull a hiking shoe out of the bag? _____

I. What is the probability that Maria will pull a sandal out of the bag? _____

J. What shoe is most likely to be pulled from the bag? _____

K. What shoe is least likely to be pulled from the bag? _____

Probability Practice

Study the example on page 79. Then, write the probability of each outcome.

A. There are 23 students in Steven's class. Twelve students have brown hair, 6 have blond hair, and 5 have black hair. One student is celebrating her birthday. What is the probability that her hair is blond?

_____

B. When Mr. Allen arrives home from work, he empties his change into a small bowl. There are 6 quarters, 3 dimes, 4 nickels, and 8 pennies. If he picks a coin out of the bowl without looking, what is the probability that he will choose a quarter?

_____

C. Lee tosses a two-sided coin (heads and tails) into the air. What is the probability it will land on heads?

_____

D. Mrs. Schultz has a bowl of fruit on her kitchen table. There are 5 bananas, 2 oranges, 3 apples, and 1 pear. What is the probability of:

picking a banana? _____

not picking a pear? _____

picking an orange or apple? _____

E. Karen has a collection of baseball cards. She has 53 cards from National League players and 61 from American League players. Without looking at them, what is the probability of choosing a card from the National League?

_____

Summer Bridge Math RB-904089

Classifying

> The words **all**, **some**, **no**, or **none** can be used when making comparisons.
>
> All dogs are animals.   All addition problems use the addition (+) sign.
> Some animals are dogs.   Some math problems use the addition sign.
> No cats are dogs.   No division problems use the addition sign.

Study the examples above. Then, complete each statement with all, some, no, or none.

A. _____ rectangles have 4 vertices. _____ rectangles are parallelograms. _____ rectangles are circles.

B. _____ even numbers end in "O." _____ even numbers end in an even number. _____ even numbers end with an odd number.

C. _____ addition problems have an answer called a "sum."

_____ addition problems have an answer called a "difference."

_____ math problems have an answer called a "sum."

D. _____ triangles have 4 vertices. _____ triangles are congruent. _____ triangles have 3 vertices.

Use the polygons to complete the statements using all, some, no, or none.

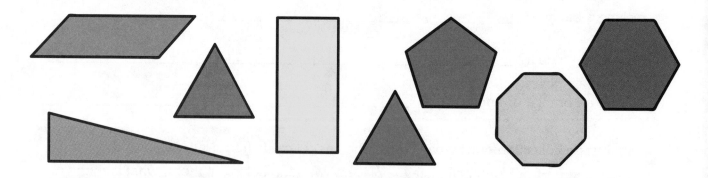

E. _____ of the polygons in this diagram have less than 3 vertices.

F. _____ polygons are congruent.

G. _____ polygons have three or more sides.

Summer Bridge Math RB-904089

Addition and Subtraction

Problem solving means using the numbers in a story to solve a math problem.

Example: Tyler drove his toy car 1,089 inches. Alexis drove her toy car 2,802 inches. How many more inches did Alexis drive her car than Tyler?

$$
\begin{array}{r}
2,8\overset{7\;9}{0}2 \\
-\ 1,089 \\
\hline
1,713
\end{array}
$$

2,802   distance Alexis drove her car
− 1,089   distance Tyler drove his car
1,713   difference in the distances

Alexis drove her car 1,713 inches more than Tyler drove his car.

Study the example above. Then, solve each problem.

A. The Toy Time toy factory made 1,492 yellow yo-yos and 4,201 red yo-yos. How many more red yo-yos were made than yellow yo-yos?

B. Sarah has 246 animal stickers and 432 flower stickers. How many stickers does Sarah have altogether?

C. The Toy Time factory made 1,648 board games, 2,190 dolls, and 4,018 race cars. How many toys did they make in all?

D. Kevin and his friends kept track of how far they flew their model airplanes. Josh flew his plane 549 feet. Annie flew hers 418 feet. Kevin flew his plane 376 feet. How many feet did their airplanes fly altogether?

E. The Toy Time Web site had 631 visitors in 1 week. If the same number of people visited their Web site each week, how many people visited the site in 3 weeks?

F. Jack has $20.00 in his pocket. He spends $1.16 playing video games and $2.59 on comic books. How much money does Jack have left?

Summer Bridge Math RB-904089

Multiplication

Study the example on page 83. Then, use multiplication to solve each problem.

A. Marcy and her friends are planning a carnival. They are planning on 3,389 people attending each day. If the carnival is open for 5 days, how many people should they plan for altogether?

B. Sidney buys prizes for the Toss-a-Ring game. She buys 15 times as many rubber balls as toy cars. If she buys 1,382 toy cars, how many rubber balls does she buy?

C. Marcy sells 1,065 gallons of orange punch. She sells 24 times as many gallons of red punch as orange punch. How many gallons of red punch does Marcy sell?

D. Andy buys 2,959 tickets for 25¢ each. What is the total amount Andy spends?

E. Ricky has 3,473 T-shirts made to sell at the carnival. He only sells 2,088 T-shirts. If he charges $5.75 for each T-shirt, how much money does he earn altogether?

F. On Monday, 2,476 people go to the carnival. The same number of people go to the carnival on Tuesday and on Wednesday. How many people go to the carnival altogether?

G. Isabella buys 4,832 pints of chocolate ice cream. If Isabella buys 28 times as many pints of vanilla ice cream as chocolate ice cream, how many pints of vanilla ice cream does she buy?

H. Travis buys 2,388 red balloons. He buys 7 times as many blue balloons as red balloons. Then, he buys 12 times as many yellow balloons as blue balloons. How many balloons does Travis buy altogether?

Summer Bridge Math RB-904089

Division

Study the example on page 83. Then, use division to solve each problem.

A. Kyle is packaging jam in cartons. If each carton holds 9 bottles of jam, how many cartons will he need to package 1,934 bottles of jam?

B. Anna has 7,209 cans of soup that need to be boxed. If she puts 9 cans of soup in 1 box, how many boxes will she need?

C. Katherine has 9,315 sunflower seeds. She puts 7 seeds in each package. How many full packages of sunflower seeds does Katherine have when she is finished? How many seeds are left over?

D. Jackson is bottling 6,488 ounces of root beer. One bottle holds 8 ounces. How many bottles will Jackson have if he bottles all of the root beer?

E. Mario is packaging footballs in a box. Six footballs will fit in one box. How many boxes will Mario need if he must package 288 footballs?

F. Katie has 2,837 flowers. If Katie puts 7 flowers in each vase, how many full vases will Katie have when she is finished? How many flowers will be left?

G. Linus is bottling soda. Each bottle holds 7 ounces. How many bottles does Linus need if he has 2,786 ounces of soda to bottle?

H. Jenny is packaging fruit. She has 349 apples, 328 pears, and 548 oranges. If she puts 4 pieces of fruit in each package, how many full packages will she have when she is finished? How many pieces of fruit will be left?

Summer Bridge Math RB-904089

Money

Study the example on page 83. Then, solve each problem.

A. Darrel bought a shirt for $19.45, a package of socks for $7.21, and sunglasses for $28.59. How much money did he spend in all?

B. At Sylvia's garage sale, she sold a bike for $25.00, a framed picture for $5.00, a stool for $4.50, and a dress for $1.75. How much did she make from those items?

C. Donna made $49.72 from babysitting jobs. She spent $14.36 on a new CD. How much did she have left over?

D. Bill and Tony collected $168.42 for the school dance. If they need $75.00 to cover the expenses for decorations and music, how much did they have left over?

E. Lynn wants to get party favors for her birthday party. Each party favor costs $2.32. She plans to invite 14 people to her party. How much will she spend on party favors for 14 people?

F. Sam and his dad invited 16 children to play putt-putt golf at the park. Each child's ticket cost $3.50. How much did their park collect for children's tickets that day?

G. Flora and her cousin washed 15 cars at the club's car wash. They charged $3.75 per car. About how much did they collect for the cars they washed? (Estimate.)

Summer Bridge Math RB-904089

Measurement

Study the example on page 83. Then, solve each problem.

A. If a room is 10 feet long, how many inches long is the room?

B. Janie wants to recarpet her hallway. The length is 11 feet. When she goes to the store, she finds that carpet is only sold by the yard. How many yards will she have to buy to have enough?

C. Mindy's banana bread recipe calls for 6 ounces of butter per loaf of bread. How many loaves of bread can she make with 2 pounds of butter?

D. An elevator has a weight limit of 1 ton. If 9 people who are riding the elevator have a combined weight of 1,800 pounds, are they under or over the limit?

E. A fruit punch recipe calls for $\frac{1}{2}$ pint of lime juice. If the recipe is tripled, how many cups of lime juice are needed?

F. Mrs. Miller is having a party for her son's birthday. She wants to have enough juice so that all 10 children can drink 2 cups. How many gallons of juice should she buy?

G. Sarah bought 54 yards of yarn to knit mittens. She had 5 yards of yarn left over. How many yards of yarn did she use to knit the mittens?

Summer Bridge Math RB-904089

Fractions

Study the example on page 83. Then, solve each problem.

A. There are 12 girls and 13 boys in Ms. Keung's class. What fraction of the class is boys?

B. Forty-three students tried out for the school play. Twenty students were selected. What fraction of the students were not selected?

C. Shirley filled one muffin cup $\frac{6}{8}$ full of muffin mix and another muffin cup $\frac{5}{8}$ full. Which muffin cup had more mix?

D. A recipe for cookies calls for two and one-half cups of flour. Write the amount of flour as a mixed number.

E. Alexa needs half of a bar of chocolate to make one glass of hot chocolate. How many glasses can she make with 4 bars of chocolate?

F. Ray had a collection of 45 baseball cards. He traded $\frac{1}{3}$ of them to Tanner. How many cards did he trade to Tanner?

G. Karen made $6\frac{1}{2}$ gallons of punch for her party. Her guests drank $4\frac{1}{2}$ gallons. How much punch did she have left?

H. Beth drinks $8\frac{1}{2}$ glasses of water a day. In 2 days, how many glasses of water does she drink?

88

Perimeter and Area

Study the example on page 83. Then, solve each problem.

A. Jeremy and his friends are building a clubhouse. The finished size is 16 feet by 24 feet. How many square feet will their clubhouse be when it is finished?

B. Chloe measures an area of the clubhouse for carpet. The area measures 49 inches by 29 inches. How much carpet will Chloe need?

C. Kevin is painting the clubhouse door blue. The door measures 9 feet by 4 feet. What is the area of the door?

D. Abby wants to put glass in the window. If the window measures 21 inches by 32 inches, what is the area of the glass she will need?

E. Marty builds a table that is 27 inches wide and 36 inches long. What is the area of the table?

F. Pam makes a tablecloth for the new table. Her tablecloth is 42 inches by 33 inches. How many yards and inches of trim will she need to go around the entire edge of the tablecloth?

G. Jeremy wants to plant grass behind the clubhouse. The area is 17 feet by 38 feet. One package of grass seed is enough to plant 200 square feet. How many packages of grass seed will Jeremy need to plant the entire area?

H. Ryan and Jeremy will paint the outside walls of the clubhouse. Two walls measure 24 feet by 11 feet. The other 2 walls measure 16 feet by 11 feet. One gallon of paint will cover 300 square feet. How many gallons of paint will they need?

Using What We Know

> Rebecca is planning a vacation trip for her family of 4 from Denver, Colorado, to San Diego, California.

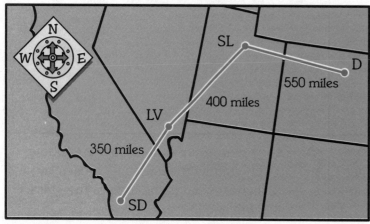

Study the example on page 83. Then, use the scenario and the map above to solve the problems.

A. If they drive, following the map above, what is their driving distance from Denver to San Diego?

B. Looking at the map above, how much farther is it from Denver to Salt Lake than from Salt Lake to Las Vegas?

C. Rebecca can buy round-trip airline tickets for $322 per ticket, or she can buy four tickets together for $1,196. How much would she save by buying the 4 tickets together?

D. If they drive, Rebecca plans on spending $250 total for two hotels (in Salt Lake and Las Vegas). She also figures it will cost $114 in gasoline to drive. Is it cheaper to drive or fly her family? How much would she save?

Real-Life Problem Solving

> The Buzzers, a local basketball team, recently played a rival team and won 84 to 82.

Study the example on page 83. Then, use the scenario above to solve each problem.

A. If Joe Johnson scored 14 points (out of the total score of 84), what fraction of the Buzzers' total points did Joe score?

B. The Buzzers made four 3-point shots. How many points were made by 3-point shots? What fraction of the points were 3-point shots?

C. The game lasted 140 minutes. If $\frac{3}{7}$ of the time was spent for time outs, how many minutes were spent in time out?

D. One-fourth of the Buzzers' points were made by Carl Malley. How many points did Carl score?

E. A college or high school basketball court is 84 feet long by 50 feet wide. A National Basketball Association court is 94 by 50 feet. What is the area of each court? What is the difference between the areas?

© Rainbow Bridge Publishing

More Real-Life Problem Solving

> Martin mows lawns in the summer for some of his neighbors. He decided to save all of his money instead of spending it.

Study the example on page 83. Then, use the scenario above to solve each problem.

A. Last summer, Martin charged his neighbors $12 each time he mowed their lawn. He earned a total of $732 over the summer. How many lawns did he mow?

B. Next year, Martin will begin fertilizing lawns. A 20-pound bag of fertilizer will be enough fertilizer for 5,000 square feet. How many square feet can each pound of fertilizer cover?

C. If Martin plans on mowing 70 lawns next summer, how much must he charge if he wants to earn $910?

D. Martin mowed 5 lawns on one Saturday at $12 per lawn. At the end of the day, he counted his money. He had $62. He remembered that Mrs. Wilson had given him a tip. How much of a tip did she give him?

E. Martin's sister Ella wants to earn some extra money next summer, too. She plans to babysit. She wants to earn $720 over the course of the summer. If Ella charges $5 an hour, how many hours will she have to babysit?

If there are 12 weeks during her summer break, how many hours a week on average will she need to work?

92
Summer Bridge Math RB-904089   © Rainbow Bridge Publishing

Answer Key

Page 7: A. 40; 4,000; 70,000;
B. 800; 1,000,000; 20,000,000;
C. 1; 80,000; 20,000;
D. 400,000,000; 70,000; 8,000;
E. 3; 200,000,000; 40,000;
F. Answers will vary.

Page 8: A. 5,621; **B.** 751,908;
C. 34,502; **D.** 89,649; **E.** 907,163;
F. 16,520; **G.** 10,080; **H.** 704,209;
I. 1,006,512; **J.** 781,250; **K.** 56,908;
L. 12,971,000; **M.** 406,230,001;
N. 64,803; **O.** 93,002

Page 9: A. 723; **B.** 9,470; **C.** 5,280;
D. 300 + 0 + 2; **E.** 604,800; **F.** 850;
G. 1,563 or 1,564

Page 10: A. 19, 13, 20, 47, 43;
B. 15, 39; **C.** 18, 27; **D.** 11, 21;
E. 17, 51; **F.** 12, 38; **G.** 23, 25;
H. 19, 25; **I.** 21, 16; **J.** 19, 22;
K. 25, 36

Page 11: A. 31, 24, 40, 25, 31, 41;
B. 54, 32, 91, 43, 23, 35; **C.** 74, 72,
91, 43, 81, 80; **D.** 34, 83, 83, 56,
80, 74; **E.** 93, 92, 80, 95, 92, 93;
F. 54, 73, 95, 55, 44, 85; **G.** 84, 74,
85, 84, 102, 98

Page 12: A. 60, 71, 116, 148, 122;
B. 419, 239, 348, 675, 537;
C. 674, 910; 1,165; 1,337; 1,071;
D. 9,511; 10,012; 7,704; 17,396;
7,983; **E.** 9,512; 14,169; 7,200;
14,455; 13,940; **F.** 27,189; 45,986;
62,245; 51,389; 72,505

Page 13: A. 9,199; 12,788; 4,714;
12,471; 5,323; **B.** 10,347; 9,530;
14,552; 11,585; 10,966; **C.** 12,264;
11,319; 7,305; 8,567; 3,782;
D. 12,731; 5,110; 7,536; 13,375;
8,031; **E.** 7,411; 18,264; 10,623;
8,037; 10,887; **F.** 89,562; 122,121;
93,467; 164,259; 79,387;
G. 51,631; 157,245; 86,384;
61,133; 110,615

Page 14: A. 1,965; 2,381; 798,
789; 1,437; **B.** 15,301; 20,660;
13,608; 22,532; 13,031; **C.** 1,203;
23,745; 18,407; 125,262; 127,881;
D. 2,365; 2,446; 19,957; 28,793;
135,110; **E.** 2,709; 13,787; 114,667;
850,878; 63,083

Page 15: A. 40, 80, 20, 60; **B.** 200,
400, 200; 3,000; **C.** 6,000; 9,000;
20,000; 50,000; **D.** 40 + 20 = 60,
80 + 20 = 100, 60 + 40 = 100,
30 + 10 = 40; **E.** 200 + 30 = 230,
800 + 100 = 900, 100 + 30 = 130,
1,000 + 300 = 1,300; **F.** 5,000 +
100 = 5,100; 300 + 600 = 900;
8,000 + 8,000 = 16,000; 20,000 +
10,000 = 30,000

Page 16: A. 67, 161, 124, 69, 282,
567; **B.** 425, 195, 288, 384, 591,
891; **C.** 183, 792, 593, 455, 872,
342; **D.** 279, 587, 399, 569, 927,
58; **E.** 52, 345, 615, 132, 487, 711;
F. 560, 467, 65, 319, 904, 673

Page 17: A. 1,063; 6,684; 1,612;
538, 791; **B.** 5,325; 2,107; 3,449;
4,841; 3,997; **C.** 80,967; 78,112;
80,946; 92,290; 60,048; **D.** 51,236;
61,911; 70,136; 31,726; 92,591;
E. 4,399; 58,527; 32,813; 1,921;
44,633; **F.** 45,434; 21,434; 5,611;
4,462; 1,264

Page 18: A. 11, 52, 122, 63;
B. 155; 2,702; 459, 548; **C.** 4,253;
411, 744; 1,532; **D.** 159, 267;
2,276; 1,268; **E.** 1,792; 1,270;
74,701; 57,658; **F.** 65,502; 11,563;
50,573; 3,711; **G.** 4,403; 81,302;
6,129; 4,018

Page 19: A. 993, 790, 929; 1,377;
1,117; 1,291; **B.** 922, 805; 1,238;
1,131; 1,041; 615; **C.** 535; 1,337;
1,451; 1,362; 1,066; 1,598; **D.** 435,
409, 222, 184, 88; 3,062; **E.** 1,217;
1,541; 522, 617; 1,770; 779;
F. 1,363; 2,438; 1,640; 2,079;
849, 981

Page 20: A. 1,919; 4,002; 7,183;
5,294; 2,560; 6,231; **B.** 4,892;
2,102; 11,493; 11,520; 9,382;
6,235; **C.** 12,268; 13,300; 7,669;
5,977; 11,686; 10,721; **D.** 2,913;
2,073; 7,233; 6,209; 1,818; 2,322;
E. 1,319; 718, 718; 4,788; 2,088;
4,455; **F.** 24,308; 59,329; 52,326;
31,741; 33,854; 74,037

Page 21: A. 54,015; 105,315;
31,600; 108,281; **B.** 151,152;
103,077; 41,340; 354,312;
C. 83,390; 71,526; 272,748;
47,664; **D.** 486,972; 96,012;
29,792; 317,952

Page 22: A. 816,775; 481,500;
593,568; 96,712; **B.** 858,364;
108,934; 130,442; 355,008;
C. 1,992,711; 2,784,960; 1,660,811;
575,190; **D.** 474,700; 1,269,576;
2,057,096; 4,772,236

Page 23: A. 40, 15; **B.** 140, 30;
C. 24, 144; **D.** 36, 40; **E.** 42, 108;
F. 30, 32; **G.** 26, 16; **H.** 3, 12; **I.** 25,
17; **J.** 55, 33

Page 24: A. 56, 27, 65, 87, 82;
B. 27, 69, 91, 47, 78; **C.** 92, 142,
191, 63, 82; **D.** 28, 43, 96, 97, 24;
E. 23, 87, 84, 68, 58

Page 25: A. 1,241; 402, 599, 654,
204; **B.** 714 r1, 922 r3, 1,028 r2,
4,308 r1, 931 r1

Answer Key

Page 26: A. 110 r2, 55, 68 r48, 67 r2; **B.** 52 r16, 59 r1, 120 r1, 420 r7; **C.** 50, 71 r10, 400 r4, 46; **D.** 16 r5, 84 r27, 51

Page 27: A. 5, 30, 20; **B.** 30, 11, 12; **C.** 50, 10, 2; **D.** 10, 10, 18; **E.** 30, 25, 50; **F.** 300, 100, 300

Page 28: A. 3, 1; **B.** 2, 1; **C.** 2, 2; **D.** 1, 5; **E.** 2, 3; **F.** 4, 11; **G.** 2, 13; **H.** 16, 17; **I.** 8, 4; **J.** 1, 10

Page 29: A. 104 r3, 318 r2, 83 r1; **B.** 1,297 r2, 563 r8, 788 r5; **C.** 988 r7, 418 r3, 1,846 r1

Page 30: A. 30, 1:00; **B.** 25, 3:00; **C.** 10, 12:00; **D.** 15, 8:00; **E.** 55, 5:00; **F.** 40, 1:00; **G.** 45, 10:00

Page 31: A. 5:35, 11:55, 5:05; **B.** 4:20, 8:30, 4:20; **C.** 6:55, 8:05; **D.** 1:55, 12:50; **E.** 2:55, 3:45; **F.** 2:45, 3:50; **G.** 2 hours

Page 32: A. 7:45; **B.** 10:15; **C.** 8:15; **D.** 10:45; **E.** 10:45; **F.** 11:45; **G.** 12:00; **H.** 1:45; **I.** 2:20 P.M.; **J.** 9:55 P.M.; **K.** 7:20 A.M.; **L.** 10:00 P.M.

Page 33: A. $6.35, $9.27; **B.** $4.42, $5.75; **C.** $7.61, $3.84; **D.** $15.22; **E.** $24.34; **F.** $57.19; **G.** $70.99; **H.** $35.29; **I.** $85.15; **J.** $1.00; **K.** $1.07; **L.** $5.17; **M.** $15.53; **N.** $60.62; **O.** $1.50

Page 34: A. $9.26, $15.93, $29.33, $36.99; **B.** $43.79, $90.16, $112.87, $280.20; **C.** $638.72, $1,158.30, $1,403.16, $803.51; **D.** $20.46, $17.27, $9.12, $40.75; **E.** $110.12, $252.99, $304.08, $476.16; **F.** $240.41, $275.33, $128.53, $290.01; **G.** $255.59, $980.68, $439.51, $994.21; **H.** $2.15

Page 35: A. $5.00 + $4.00 = $9.00, $9.00 + $6.00 = $15.00, $8.00 + $5.00 = $13.00, $15.00 + $13.00 = $28.00; **B.** $28.00 + $17.00 = $45.00, $57.00 + $39.00 = $96.00, $10.00 – $5.00 = $5.00, $11.00 – $5.00 = $6.00; **C.** $19.00 – $12.00 = $7.00, $23.00 – $19.00 = $4.00, $50.00 – $31.00 = $19.00, $78.00 – $57.00 = $21.00; **D.** $8.00 x 4 = $32.00, $16.00 x 3 = $48.00, $26.00 x 5 = $130.00, $43.00 x 9 = $387.00; **E.** $24.00 ÷ 6 = $4.00, $40.00 ÷ 8 = $5.00, $9.00 ÷ 3 = $3.00, $10.00 ÷ 5 = $2.00

Page 36: A. 2, 72, 24; **B.** 6, 5,280, 15; **C.** 48, 9, 5; **D.** 2, 18, 60; **E.** 84, 10, 7,040; **F.** 14 yards of string; **G.** 4 yards of ribbon; **H.** 18 feet of fabric; **I.** 66 inches tall

Page 37: A. 3 cm, 2 cm; **B.** 6 cm, 4 cm; **C.** 1 cm, 5 cm; **D.** 3,000; 50, 200; **E.** 30, 2, 5; **F.** 3; 5,000; 4; **G.** 70; 250; 3,500; **H.** 2 m, 3 cm

Page 38: A. 8, 10, 64; **B.** 28, 12, 17; **C.** 64, 8, 36; **D.** 30, 30, 44; **E.** 2, 12, 7; **F.** 14 pints of water; **G.** 24 cups of fruit; **H.** 7 gallons of hot chocolate; **I.** 116 bottles

Page 39: A. mL, L, L; **B.** mL, L, mL; **C.** L, mL, mL; **D.** 2,000; 3, 9; **E.** 2,500; 6,700; 3.5; **F.** 7; 5,000; 4,500; **G.** mL; **H.** L; **I.** mL

Page 40: A. tons, ounces; **B.** ounces, tons; **C.** pounds, ounces; **D.** pounds, tons; **E.** <, =; **F.** >, <; **G.** =, <; **H.** =, =; **I.** 142 pounds and 1 ounce

Page 41: A. kg, g, kg; **B.** kg, g, g; **C.** 4,000; 5; **D.** 6,000; 6.5; **E.** 9; 4,500; **F.** 20; 7,000; **G.** 7.5; 1,500; **H.** 12; 11,000; **I.** 150 dimes

Page 42: A. 2, 35, 108; **B.** 2, 480, 7; **C.** 2, 5, 63; **D.** 300, 180; 2,400; **E.** 84, 42, 4; **F.** 28 days; **G.** 4 weeks; **H.** 8 hours; **I.** 10 hours and 30 minutes or 10.5 hours

Page 43: A. $\frac{5}{6}$; **B.** $\frac{1}{8}$; **C.** $\frac{2}{3}$; **D.** $\frac{4}{8}$; **E.** $\frac{16}{32}$; **F.** $\frac{3}{12}$; **G.** $\frac{2}{5}$; **H.** $\frac{3}{8}$

Page 44: A. $\frac{3}{5}$, $\frac{3}{4}$; **B.** $\frac{4}{9}$, $\frac{1}{4}$; **C.** $\frac{1}{3}$, $\frac{6}{12}$; **D.** $\frac{2}{8}$, $\frac{4}{10}$; **E.** $\frac{4}{5}$, $\frac{5}{11}$; **F.** $\frac{1}{2}$, $\frac{7}{8}$; **G.** one-third, two-thirds; **H.** one-half, one-eighth; **I.** three-eighths, four-elevenths; **J.** two-fifths, five-thirds; **K.** five-sevenths, five-ninths; **L.** four-thirds, nine-halves

Page 45: A. $\frac{1}{2}$, $\frac{2}{5}$, $\frac{1}{3}$; **B.** $\frac{2}{3}$, $\frac{1}{3}$, $\frac{3}{5}$; **C.** $\frac{3}{4}$, $\frac{1}{12}$, $\frac{2}{3}$; **D.** $\frac{1}{3}$, $\frac{1}{4}$, $\frac{5}{6}$; **E.** $\frac{1}{2}$, $\frac{1}{4}$, $\frac{1}{1}$ or 1

Page 46: A. $\frac{4}{8}$, $\frac{3}{6}$; **B.** $\frac{2}{6}$, $\frac{8}{16}$; **C.** 12, 3, 10; **D.** 12, 1, 6

Page 47: A. LCD = 15, $\frac{10}{15}$, $\frac{12}{15}$; **B.** LCD = 6, $\frac{3}{6}$, $\frac{2}{6}$; **C.** LCD = 10, $\frac{4}{10}$, $\frac{5}{10}$; **D.** LCD = 20, $\frac{15}{20}$, $\frac{4}{20}$; **E.** LCD = 21, $\frac{14}{21}$; **F.** LCD = 21, $\frac{18}{21}$, $\frac{7}{21}$; **G.** LCD = 10, $\frac{5}{10}$, $\frac{6}{10}$; **H.** LCD = 14, $\frac{8}{14}$, $\frac{7}{14}$; **I.** LCD = 24, $\frac{16}{24}$, $\frac{15}{24}$

Page 48: A. $\frac{3}{2}$, $1\frac{1}{2}$; **B.** $\frac{11}{6}$, $1\frac{5}{6}$; **C.** $\frac{6}{5}$, $1\frac{1}{5}$; **D.** $\frac{7}{3}$, $2\frac{1}{3}$; **E.** $\frac{11}{4}$, $2\frac{3}{4}$; **F.** $\frac{17}{6}$, $2\frac{5}{6}$

Page 49: A. $1\frac{1}{4}$, $3\frac{1}{3}$, $1\frac{1}{8}$, $2\frac{2}{3}$; **B.** $2\frac{1}{2}$, $1\frac{3}{4}$, 3, $1\frac{1}{10}$; **C.** $1\frac{3}{7}$, $2\frac{3}{8}$, $1\frac{4}{5}$, $3\frac{1}{10}$; **D.** $2\frac{3}{10}$, $2\frac{1}{8}$, $4\frac{1}{3}$, $2\frac{1}{12}$; **E.** $3\frac{1}{9}$, $2\frac{1}{4}$, $2\frac{1}{6}$, $3\frac{1}{25}$

Page 50: A. $2\frac{1}{2}$, $3\frac{1}{3}$, $2\frac{2}{3}$; **B.** $1\frac{2}{3}$, $6\frac{1}{2}$, 7; **C.** $2\frac{1}{4}$, $4\frac{1}{3}$, $6\frac{1}{2}$; **D.** 7, $5\frac{1}{4}$, $3\frac{1}{2}$

Page 51: A. $\frac{11}{15}$, $\frac{17}{24}$, $\frac{5}{6}$, $1\frac{7}{20}$; **B.** $1\frac{7}{30}$, $\frac{20}{21}$, $\frac{19}{30}$, $1\frac{1}{18}$; **C.** $\frac{25}{28}$, $\frac{23}{24}$, $1\frac{1}{12}$, $1\frac{11}{30}$

Page 52: A. $4\frac{1}{8}$, $2\frac{2}{3}$, $5\frac{2}{9}$, $3\frac{3}{5}$; **B.** $7\frac{1}{5}$, $4\frac{5}{9}$, $11\frac{8}{11}$, $8\frac{1}{9}$; **C.** $6\frac{2}{3}$, $9\frac{4}{5}$, $11\frac{3}{10}$, $7\frac{1}{6}$

Answer Key

Page 53: A. $5\frac{2}{3}$, $4\frac{3}{5}$, 6, $13\frac{1}{2}$;
B. $6\frac{1}{5}$, $14\frac{1}{8}$, $4\frac{1}{2}$, $6\frac{3}{7}$; **C.** 13, $6\frac{1}{3}$,
$4\frac{1}{10}$, $4\frac{4}{5}$

Page 54: A. $1\frac{5}{7}$, $2\frac{2}{3}$, $\frac{1}{3}$, $5\frac{3}{4}$; **B.** $2\frac{3}{5}$,
$\frac{3}{5}$, $2\frac{3}{5}$, $2\frac{5}{6}$; **C.** $\frac{1}{2}$, $\frac{2}{3}$, $1\frac{5}{6}$, $5\frac{1}{2}$

Page 55: A. $\frac{3}{8}$, $\frac{2}{15}$, $\frac{2}{15}$, $\frac{5}{12}$, $\frac{3}{32}$; **B.** $\frac{5}{24}$, $\frac{5}{14}$,
$\frac{1}{12}$, $\frac{2}{25}$, $\frac{3}{10}$; **C.** $\frac{3}{32}$, $\frac{6}{25}$, $\frac{1}{4}$, $\frac{4}{9}$, $\frac{3}{16}$; **D.** $\frac{5}{21}$, $\frac{3}{14}$,
$\frac{5}{24}$, $\frac{5}{18}$, $\frac{3}{35}$

Page 56: A. 2, $1\frac{3}{5}$, $\frac{6}{7}$, $1\frac{1}{7}$;
B. $2\frac{2}{5}$, $\frac{9}{10}$, $6\frac{3}{4}$, $1\frac{4}{5}$; **C.** $1\frac{1}{3}$, $1\frac{5}{7}$,
$1\frac{1}{2}$, $1\frac{1}{2}$; **D.** $1\frac{1}{2}$, $1\frac{1}{9}$, $\frac{7}{9}$, $2\frac{2}{3}$

Page 57: A. 10, $3\frac{1}{8}$, $4\frac{19}{20}$; **B.** $2\frac{6}{25}$,
$8\frac{1}{3}$, $7\frac{1}{2}$; **C.** $5\frac{13}{24}$, $2\frac{1}{4}$, $1\frac{27}{28}$; **D.** $6\frac{3}{10}$,
$5\frac{1}{2}$, $6\frac{3}{4}$

Page 58: A. $\frac{2}{10}$, 0.2; **B.** $\frac{8}{10}$, 0.8;
C. $\frac{9}{10}$, 0.9; **D.** $\frac{1}{10}$, 0.1; **E.** $\frac{13}{100}$, 0.13;
F. $\frac{87}{100}$, 0.87; **G.** $\frac{55}{100}$, 0.55

Page 59: A. $\frac{3}{10}$; **B.** one and twelve
hundredths, $1\frac{12}{100}$; **C.** 0.221, $\frac{221}{1000}$;
D. 0.53, fifty-three hundredths;
E. eight hundred seventy-one
thousandths, $\frac{871}{1000}$; **F.** 2.01, two and
one hundredth

Page 60: A. 0.1, 0.7, 0.06; **B.** 0.11,
2.2, 0.9; **C.** 1.05, 5.6, 5.06;
D. 0.86, 0.19, 0.12; **E.** eight-tenths;
F. eight-hundredths; **G.** three and
five-hundredths; **H.** fifty-three
hundredths; **I.** five and fifty-three
hundredths; **J.** one and fourteen-
hundredths; **K.** nine-tenths;
L. one-hundredth; **M.** three and
twenty-eight hundredths

Page 61: A. <, <; **B.** <, >; **C.** >, >;
D. >, >; **E.** <, <; **F.** <, =; **G.** <, >;
H. =, <

Page 62: A. 0.5, 0.03, 0.45; **B.** 0.9,
0.25, 0.6; **C.** 0.76, 0.2, 0.4; **D.** $\frac{67}{100}$, $\frac{3}{10}$,
$\frac{81}{100}$; **E.** $\frac{73}{100}$, $\frac{55}{100}$, $\frac{6}{10}$; **F.** $\frac{5}{100}$, $\frac{33}{100}$, $\frac{8}{10}$;
G. <, <, <

Page 63: A. 2.9, 12.19; **B.** 5.10, 3.2;
C. 6.42, 9.6; **D.** 12.12, 1.51; **E.** nine
and one-tenth, seven-hundredths;
F. four-tenths, five and ninety-nine
hundredths; **G.** ten and one-
hundredth, thirty-two hundredths;
H. five and six-tenths, eleven and
eleven-hundredths

Page 64: A. 4.4, 0.23; **B.** 1.03, 0.5;
C. 0.548, 2.53; **D.** 53.17, 16.303;
E. 0.091, 91.3; **F.** $2\frac{87}{100}$, $\frac{983}{1000}$; **G.** $14\frac{5}{10}$,
$287\frac{69}{100}$; **H.** $1\frac{752}{1000}$, $\frac{7}{10}$; **I.** $\frac{6}{100}$, $10\frac{54}{1000}$;
J. $81\frac{2}{10}$, $\frac{157}{1000}$

Page 65: A. pentagon,
quadrilateral; **B.** triangle, heptagon;
C. pentagon, octagon

Page 66: A. a., c., d.; a., c.; **B.** a.,
b.; a., c.; **C.** a., b.; a., c., e.

Page 67: A. 6, 12; **B.** 5, 9; **C.** 6, 12;
D. 8, 18; **E.** 14, 34

Page 68: A. congruent, similar;
B. congruent, similar;
C. similar, similar

Page 69: A. 3, 1, 4; **B.** 4, 1, 1; **C.** 0,
1, 1; **D.** 4, 4, 1; Lines of symmetry
should be drawn correctly.

Page 70: A. $\overrightarrow{BA}$; **B.** Point X; **C.** $\overline{JK}$ or
$\overline{KJ}$; **D.** Point M; **E.** $\overleftrightarrow{OP}$ or $\overleftrightarrow{PO}$;
F. $\overrightarrow{YX}$; **G.** $\overline{ST}$ or $\overline{TS}$; **H.** Point J; **I.** $\overleftrightarrow{LM}$
or $\overleftrightarrow{ML}$; **J.** $\overrightarrow{CD}$; **K.** $\overleftrightarrow{QR}$ or $\overleftrightarrow{RQ}$; **L.** $\overline{BC}$ or
$\overline{CB}$; **M.** $\overline{AB}$, $\overline{BC}$, $\overline{CD}$, $\overrightarrow{DE}$

Page 71: A. acute; **B.** obtuse;
C. right; **D.** obtuse; **E.** acute;
F. obtuse; **G.** right; **H.** acute;
I. obtuse; **J.** acute; **K.** right; **L.** right

Page 72: A. 4, 4; **B.** pentagon, 5;
C. 6; **D.** 7, 7; **E.** octagon, 8;
F. square; **G.** rectangle; **H.** circle;
I. triangle; **J.** trapezoid; **K.**
pentagon; **L.** parallelogram

Page 73: A. 32 in.; **B.** 25 cm;
C. 58 yd.; **D.** 32 m; **E.** 24 cm;
F. 41 m; **G.** 40 in.; **H.** 76 ft.

Page 74: A. 12, 25; **B.** 20, 84;
C. 18; **D.** 4; **E.** 30; **F.** 15; **G.** 5

Page 75:
A. 9 choices

mountain — red / blue / purple

road — red / blue / purple

BMX — red / blue / purple

B. 10 choices

Eva — hot dog / hamburger

Friend 1 — hot dog / hamburger

Friend 2 — hot dog / hamburger

Friend 3 — hot dog / hamburger

Friend 4 — hot dog / hamburger

© Rainbow Bridge Publishing

Summer Bridge Math RB-904089

Answer Key

Page 75 (continued)
C. 10 choices

1.5 " — red, blue, black, green, brown

2 " — red, blue, black, green, brown

D. 4 choices

apples — red, green

grapes — red, green

E. 25 choices

Group 1 — lima beans, string beans, yellow squash, corn, watermelon

Group 2 — lima beans, string beans, yellow squash, corn, watermelon

Group 3 — lima beans, string beans, yellow squash, corn, watermelon

Group 4 — lima beans, string beans, yellow squash, corn, watermelon

Group 5 — lima beans, string beans, yellow squash, corn, watermelon

Page 76: A. 10, 5, 3, 4; **B.** dog; **C.** fish; **D.** 2; **E.** December; **F.** November; **G.** 2,200; **H.** Answers will vary.

Page 77: A. 1:30 P.M.; **B.** 10:45 P.M.; **C.** 7:15 P.M.; **D.** 101; **E.** 2 hours and 30 minutes or 2.5 hours; **F.** 3:45 P.M.; **G.** 104; **H.** 103 and 106; **I.** 102; **J.** 106

Page 78: A. 20, 60, 40; **B.** 5, –10, 30; **C.** 100, 80, 10

Page 79: A. $\frac{2}{11}$; **B.** $\frac{1}{11}$; **C.** $\frac{3}{11}$; **D.** $\frac{0}{11}$ or none; **E.** $\frac{5}{11}$; **F.** yellow

Page 80: A. less likely; **B.** more likely; **C.** impossible; **D.** less likely; **E.** certain; **F.** $\frac{10}{24}$; **G.** $\frac{2}{24}$; **H.** $\frac{4}{24}$; **I.** $\frac{8}{24}$; **J.** sneaker; **K.** dress shoe

Page 81: A. $\frac{6}{23}$; **B.** $\frac{6}{21}$; **C.** $\frac{1}{2}$; **D.** $\frac{5}{11}, \frac{10}{11}, \frac{5}{11}$; **E.** $\frac{53}{114}$

Page 82: A. all, all, no; **B.** some, all, no; **C.** all, no, some; **D.** no, some, all; **E.** none; **F.** some; **G.** all

Page 83: A. 2,709 more red yo-yos; **B.** 678 stickers; **C.** 7,856 toys; **D.** 1,343 feet; **E.** 1,893 people; **F.** $16.25

Page 84: A. 16,945 people; **B.** 20,730 balls; **C.** 25,560 gallons of red punch; **D.** $739.75; **E.** $12,006.00; **F.** 7,428 people; **G.** 135,296 pints of vanilla ice cream; **H.** 200,592 balloons

Page 85: A. 215 cartons; **B.** 801 boxes; **C.** 1,330 packages, 5 seeds left over; **D.** 811 bottles; **E.** 48 boxes; **F.** 405 vases, 2 flowers left over; **G.** 398 bottles; **H.** 306 packages, 1 piece of fruit left over

Page 86: A. $55.25; **B.** $36.25; **C.** $35.36; **D.** $93.42; **E.** $32.48; **F.** $56.00; **G.** approximately $60.00

Page 87: A. 120 inches; **B.** 34 yards of carpet; **C.** 5 loaves of bread; **D.** under; **E.** 3 cups of lime juice; **F.** 2 gallons of juice; **G.** 49 yards of yarn

Page 88: A. $\frac{13}{25}$; **B.** $\frac{23}{43}$; **C.** $\frac{6}{8}$; **D.** $2\frac{1}{2}$; **E.** 8 glasses of hot chocolate; **F.** 15 cards; **G.** 2 gallons of punch; **H.** 17 glasses of water

Page 89: A. 384 square feet; **B.** 1,421 square inches; **C.** 36 square feet; **D.** 672 square inches; **E.** 972 inches; **F.** 4 yards and 6 inches; **G.** 4 packages of seed; **H.** 3 gallons of paint

Page 90: A. 1,300 miles; **B.** 150 miles; **C.** $92.00; **D.** drive, $832.00

Page 91: A. $\frac{1}{6}$; **B.** 12, $\frac{1}{7}$; **C.** 60; **D.** 21 points; **E.** NBA = 4,700 square feet, college/high school = 4,200 square feet, 500 square feet

Page 92: A. 61 lawns; **B.** 250 square feet; **C.** $13.00; **D.** $2.00; **E.** 144 hours, 12 hours

 Summer Bridge Math RB-904089 © Rainbow Bridge Publishing